編者的話

　　「閱讀測驗」是各類型考試的必考題型，但是一般傳統的閱讀測驗，文章都很長，再搭配數個題目，每個題目有四個選項，選項裡還有生字，看一題就要看很久，同學練習起來非常辛苦。

　　為此，我們特別設計了「極簡高中閱讀測驗」，一篇文章節選一段，文字精簡沒有廢話，每段只有一個題目，而且選項減成二個，讓你學習沒有負擔。請看下面的例子：

傳統高中閱讀測驗

〔2019 高考江蘇卷試題第一段〕

　　In the 1960s, while studying the volcanic history of Yellowstone National Park, Bob Christiansen became puzzled about something that, oddly, had not troubled anyone before: he couldn't find the park's volcano. It had been known for a long time that Yellowstone was volcanic in nature—that's what accounted for all its hot springs and other steamy features. But Christiansen couldn't find the Yellowstone volcano anywhere.

1. What puzzled Christiansen when he was studying Yellowstone?
   A. Its complicated geographical features.
   B. Its ever-lasting influence on tourism.
   C. The mysterious history of the park.
   D. The exact location of the volcano. 　【D】

你看上面這篇文章，光一段就這麼多，句子冗長又複雜，同學讀完已經頭暈腦漲，等到看題目時，早就忘了前面讀過什麼，這樣同學練習時很浪費時間，挫折感也很深，可能會對英文失去信心。原來的文章經過我們去蕪存菁，把不重要的部分刪除，題目也只留下二個選項，變成下面這樣：

極簡高中閱讀測驗

　　While studying the volcanic history of Yellowstone National Park, Bob Christiansen became puzzled. It had been known for a long time that the park was volcanic in nature, but he couldn't find the volcano.

1. What puzzled Christiansen when he was studying Yellowstone?
   A. The mysterious history of the park.
   B. The exact location of the volcano.　　　　【B】

　　你看，這樣是不是真的輕鬆許多？本書收錄100篇極簡閱讀測驗，試題均取材自大陸高考試題，改編後的文章淺顯易懂，單字及專有名詞皆有註解說明，保證你一看就懂。你還可以把文章當成練習朗讀的教材，鍛鍊自己的發音和演講實力，一舉數得。本書的目標，就是讓同學在短時間內，提升英文程度，你會越做越有精神，做完100篇極簡閱測之後，任何閱讀測驗都難不倒你了。

　　本書雖經審慎校對，仍恐有疏漏之處，煩請各界先進不吝批評指教。

劉毅

TEST 1

【2019 高考江蘇卷】

用手機掃瞄聽錄音

While studying the volcanic history of Yellowstone National Park, Bob Christiansen became puzzled. It had been known for a long time that the park was volcanic in nature, but he couldn't find the volcano.

1. What puzzled Christiansen when he was studying Yellowstone?
   A. The mysterious history of the park.
   B. The exact location of the volcano.

TEST 1 詳解

【2019 高考江蘇卷】

While studying the volcanic history of Yellowstone National

Park, Bob Christiansen became puzzled. It had been known
　　　　　　　　　　　　　　　　　　　　　　　　　　虛主詞

for a long time *that the park was volcanic in nature*, *but* he
　　　　　　　　　　　　　眞　正　主　詞

couldn't find the volcano.

　　在研究美國黃石國家公園火山的歷史時，鮑伯‧克里斯辰森感到非常困惑。長久以來大家都知道，這座國家公園是天然的火山地形，但是他找不到火山。

> * volcanic〔val'kænɪk〕*adj.* 火山的
> Bob Christiansen〔'bɑb 'krɪtʃənsən〕*n.* 鮑伯‧克里斯辰森
> puzzled〔'pʌzl̩d〕*adj.* 困惑的　　*in nature* 本質上；自然上
> volcano〔val'keno〕*n.* 火山

1.(**B**) What puzzled Christiansen when he was studying Yellowstone?

　　當克里斯辰森在研究黃石公園時，什麼事情使他很困惑？

　　(A) The mysterious history of the park.
　　　　這座公園神秘的歷史。

　　(B) The exact location of the volcano. 火山的正確位置。

> * puzzle〔'pʌzl̩〕*v.* 使困惑
> mysterious〔mɪs'tɪrɪəs〕*adj.* 神祕的
> exact〔ɪg'zækt〕*adj.* 正確的
> location〔lo'keʃən〕*n.* 位置

TEST 2

【2019 高考北京卷】

The oceans will be bluer and greener thanks to a warming climate. Tiny marine organisms called phytoplankton create colorful patterns at the ocean surface. Ocean color varies from green to blue, depending on the type and concentration of it. Climate change will stimulate its growth in some areas, while reducing it in other spots, leading to changes in the ocean's appearance.

1. What is the paragraph mainly about?

   A. The various patterns at the ocean surface.

   B. The cause of the changes in ocean color.

TEST 3

【2019 高考天津卷】

When a predator always eats a single prey, the two species are strongly linked; when a predator lives on various species, they are weakly linked. If a predator can eat several species, it can survive the extinction of one of them. Food webs dominated by many weak links are more stable.

1. A strong link is found between two species when a predator _____.

　A. has a wide food choice

　B. sticks to one prey species

TEST 2 詳解

【2019 高考北京卷】

The oceans will be bluer and greener *thanks to a warming*

climate. Tiny marine organisms *called phytoplankton* create

colorful patterns *at the ocean surface.* Ocean color varies

from green to blue, *depending on the type and concentration of it.*

Climate change will stimulate its growth *in some areas,* **while**

reducing it *in other spots, leading to changes in the ocean's*

appearance.

　　由於氣候逐漸暖化，海洋將會更藍、更綠。被稱為浮游植物的微小海洋生物，會在海洋表面製造出多色彩的圖案。海洋的顏色從綠色到藍色各有不同，視浮游植物的種類和濃度而定。氣候改變在有些地區會刺激浮游植物的生長，而在有些地區則會使它減少，造成海洋外觀的變化。

　　* ***thanks to*** 因為；由於　　climate〔ˋklaɪmɪt〕*n.* 氣候
　　tiny〔ˋtaɪnɪ〕*adj.* 微小的　　marine〔məˋrin〕*adj.* 海洋的
　　organism〔ˋɔrgənˏɪzəm〕*n.* 有機體；生物
　　phytoplankton〔ˏfaɪtoˋplæŋktən〕*n.* 浮游植物
　　create〔krɪˋet〕*v.* 創造；製造

pattern〔'pætən〕*n.* 花樣；圖案　　surface〔'sɜfɪs〕*n.* 表面

vary〔'vɛrɪ〕*v.* 變化；不同　　***depend on*** 視～而定

type〔taɪp〕*n.* 種類　　concentration〔,kɑnsṇ'treʃən〕*n.* 濃度

stimulate〔'stɪmjə,let〕*v.* 刺激

growth〔groθ〕*n.* 生長　　reduce〔rɪ'djus〕*v.* 減少

spot〔spɑt〕*n.* 地點　　***lead to*** 造成；導致

appearance〔ə'pɪrəns〕*n.* 外表；外觀

1.(**B**) What is the paragraph mainly about?

這個段落主要關於什麼？

(A) The various patterns at the ocean surface.

海洋表面的各種圖案。

(B) The cause of the changes in ocean color.

<u>海洋顏色改變的原因。</u>

* paragraph〔'pærə,græf〕*n.* 段落

various〔'vɛrɪəs〕*adj.* 各種的　　cause〔kɔz〕*n.* 原因

TEST 3 詳解

【2019 高考天津卷】

***When** a predator always eats a single prey*, the two species

are *strongly* linked; ***when** a predator lives on various species*,

they are *weakly* linked. ***If** a predator can eat several species*, it can survive the extinction *of one of them.* Food webs (*which*

are) *dominated by many weak links* are *more* stable.

　當掠食者總是吃單一種獵物的時候，這兩種物種就有強烈的關連；當掠食者以多種不同的物種爲食時，牠們的關連就很微弱。如果掠食者可以吃數種動物，就算其中一種絕種了，牠也可以存活。由許多微弱的關連所支配的食物網絡，是比較穩定的。

* predator〔ˋprɛdətɚ〕*n.* 掠食者　　single〔ˋsɪŋg!〕*adj.* 單一的
prey〔pre〕*n.* 獵物　　species〔ˋspiʃɪz〕*n.* 物種【單複數同形】
strongly〔ˋstrɔŋlɪ〕*adv.* 強烈地；牢固地
link〔lɪŋk〕*v., n.* 連結；關聯　　***live on*** 以～爲食
various〔ˋvɛrɪəs〕*adj.* 各種不同的
weakly〔ˋwiklɪ〕*adv.* 微弱地　　survive〔səˋvaɪv〕*v.* 存活
extinction〔ɪkˋstɪŋkʃən〕*n.* 滅絕；絕種
web〔wɛb〕*n.* 網站；網絡
dominate〔ˋdɑməˌnet〕*v.* 支配；控制
weak〔wik〕*adj.* 微弱的　　stable〔ˋsteb!〕*adj.* 穩定的

1. (**B**) A strong link is found between two species when
a predator _____.
　當掠食者 _____ 時，這兩個物種就建立起一種堅固的關聯。
(A) has a wide food choice 有廣泛的食物選擇
(B) sticks to one prey species 堅持一種獵物

* strong〔strɔŋ〕*adj.* 強烈的；牢固的
wide〔waɪd〕*adj.* 廣泛的　　choice〔tʃɔɪs〕*n.* 選擇
stick〔stɪk〕*v.* 堅持 < *to* >

TEST 4

【2019 高考北京卷】

Alice Moore is a teenager who set up a business. Her company was very successful because of the invention of a sweet treat, CanCandy, that could save kids' teeth, instead of destroying them.

1. What's special about CanCandy?
   A. It's beneficial to dental health.
   B. It's harmful to kids' teeth.

TEST 4 詳解

【2019 高考北京卷】

Alice Moore is a teenager **_who_** _set up a business._ Her company was _very_ successful _because of the invention of a sweet treat, CanCandy,_ **_that_** _could save kids' teeth,_ **_instead of_** _destroying them._

　　愛麗斯・摩爾是一位自行創業的青少年。她的公司很成功，因為發明了一種甜甜的美食，CanCandy，它可以解救孩子們的牙齒，而非毀壞它們。

　　* Alice Moore〔ˈælɪsˈmor〕*n.* 愛麗斯・摩爾
　　teenager〔ˈtinˌedʒɚ〕*n.* 十幾歲的青少年　　***set up*** 建立
　　business〔ˈbɪznɪs〕*n.* 事業　　company〔ˈkʌmpənɪ〕*n.* 公司
　　successful〔səkˈsɛsfəl〕*adj.* 成功的
　　invention〔ɪnˈvɛnʃən〕*n.* 發明　　treat〔trit〕*n.* 美食
　　save〔sev〕*v.* 解救　　kid〔kɪd〕*n.* 小孩
　　instead of 而非　　destroy〔dɪˈstrɔɪ〕*v.* 破壞

1. (**A**) What's special about CanCandy?
　　CanCandy 的特別之處是什麼？

　　(A) It's beneficial to dental health. 它對牙齒健康有益。

　　(B) It's harmful to kids' teeth. 它對小孩的牙齒有害。

　　　* beneficial〔ˌbɛnəˈfɪʃəl〕*adj.* 有益的
　　　dental〔ˈdɛntl̩〕*adj.* 牙齒的　　health〔hɛlθ〕*n.* 健康
　　　harmful〔ˈhɑrmfəl〕*adj.* 有害的

TEST 5

【2019 高考江蘇卷】

The international community worries about the "digital divide" between rich and poor countries. Thus, money is donated to developing countries to buy computers and Internet facilities. The question, however, is whether this is what they need most. Perhaps giving money for things such as digging wells would improve their lives more.

1. The paragraph suggests that donors should
   A. take people's essential needs into account.
   B. provide more affordable Internet facilities.

TEST 6

【2019 高考北京卷】

One day Moore visited a bank with her dad. She was offered a candy bar, but he reminded her that sweets were bad for her teeth. She thought, "Why can't I make a healthy candy that's good for my teeth so that my parents can't say no to it?" She wondered if she could start her own candy company. Her dad recommended that she do some research and talk to dentists.

1. How did Moore react to her dad's warning?
   A. She argued with him.
   B. She tried to find a way around it.

TEST 5 詳解

【2019 高考江蘇卷】

The international community worries about the "digital divide" *between rich and poor countries.* *Thus*, money is donated to developing countries *to buy computers and Internet facilities.* The question, *however*, is **whether** *this is* **what** *they*

名詞子句做主詞補語

need most. *Perhaps* giving money for things *such as digging*

————————————— 主詞 —————————————

wells would improve their lives *more.*

國際社會擔憂富國和窮國之間的數位差距，因此，捐款給開發中國家，購買電腦和網路設備。然而，問題在於，這是否是他們最需要的。或許，捐款來做像挖水井這些事情，更加能改善他們的生活。

* international〔͵ɪntɚˋnæʃənḷ〕*adj.* 國際的
  community〔kəˋmjunətɪ〕*n.* 社區；社會
  worry about 擔憂；擔心　　digital〔ˋdɪdʒɪtḷ〕*adj.* 數位的
  divide〔dəˋvaɪd〕*n.* 分割；分界；此指「差距」
  thus〔ðʌs〕*adv.* 因此　　donate〔ˋdonet〕*v.* 捐贈
  develop〔dɪˋvɛləp〕*v.* 發展；開發
  developing country 開發中國家
  Internet〔ˋɪntɚ͵nɛt〕*n.* 網際網路

facility〔fəˋsɪlətɪ〕*n.* 設備　　whether〔ˋhwɛðɚ〕*conj.* 是否

perhaps〔pɚˋhæps〕*adv.* 或許　　dig〔dɪg〕*v.* 挖；掘

well〔wɛl〕*n.* 井　　improve〔ɪmˋpruv〕*v.* 改善

1.(**A**) The paragraph suggests that donors should
　　　這個段落建議捐贈者應該

　　(A) take people's essential needs into account.
　　　　將人們必要的需求列入考慮。

　　(B) provide more affordable Internet facilities.
　　　　提供更多負擔得起的網路設備。

　　* paragraph〔ˋpærəˏgræf〕*n.* 段落

　　　suggest〔səˋdʒɛst〕*v.* 建議　　donor〔ˋdonɚ〕*n.* 捐贈者

　　　essential〔əˋsɛnʃəl〕*adj.* 不可缺少的；必要的

　　　account〔əˋkaʊnt〕*n.* 考慮

　　　take…into account 把…列入考慮

　　　provide〔prəˋvaɪd〕*v.* 供給；提供

　　　affordable〔əˋfordəbḷ〕*adj.* 負擔得起的

TEST 6 詳解

【2019 高考北京卷】

One day Moore visited a bank *with her dad*. She was

offered a candy bar, *but* he reminded her *that sweets were bad*

for her teeth. She thought, "Why can't I make a healthy candy *that*'s good for my teeth **so that** my parents can't say no to it?"

She wondered ***if*** she could start her own candy company. Her
   V.   —— 名詞子句做受詞 ——

dad recommended ***that*** she (*should*) do some research **and** talk
      V.   —— 名詞子句做受詞 ——

to dentists.

    有一天摩爾和她爸爸一起去銀行。人家給她一支棒棒糖，但他提醒她甜食對牙齒不好。她心想，「我為何不能做出一種健康的，對牙齒好的糖果，那我爸媽就不會說不可以了。」她想知道她是否可以創立自己的糖果公司。她爸爸建議她做一些研究，和牙醫談一談。

> * visit〔ˈvɪzɪt〕*v.* 拜訪　　offer〔ˈɔfɚ〕*v.* 提供
> bar〔bɑr〕*n.* 棒　　　remind〔rɪˈmaɪnd〕*v.* 提醒
> healthy〔ˈhɛlθɪ〕*adj.* 健康的　　***so that*** 為了；所以；因此
> wonder〔ˈwʌndɚ〕*v.* 想知道
> recommend〔ˌrɛkəˈmɛnd〕*v.* 推薦；建議
> research〔ˈrisɝtʃ〕*n.* 研究　　dentist〔ˈdɛntɪst〕*n.* 牙醫

1. (**B**) How did Moore react to her dad's warning?
摩爾對她父親的警告反應如何？

    (A) She argued with him. 她和他爭論。

    (B) She tried to find a way around it.

        她試圖找出解決辦法。

> * react〔rɪˈækt〕*v.* 反應 < *to* >
> warning〔ˈwɔrnɪŋ〕*n.* 警告
> argue〔ˈɑrgju〕*v.* 爭論 < *with sb.* >
> ***way around*** 出路；解決辦法

TEST 7

【2019 高考天津卷】

When learning to read, we start off with sentences, then paragraphs, and then stories. It seemed an unending journey, but as a little girl I realized knowing how to read could open many doors. My progress in reading raised my curiosity. I often told my mom to drive slowly so that I could read all the road signs we passed.

1. According to the paragraph, the author's reading of road signs indicates

   A. her unique way to locate herself.

   B. her eagerness to develop her reading ability.

TEST 8

【2019 高考全國卷】

Marian Bechtel sits by herself, quietly reading her e-book as she waits for her salad. Lunch outside the office is her "me" time. She works through lunch at her desk very often. A lunchtime escape prevents her boss from interrupting her. She returns to work feeling energized. "I prefer to be out alone. I just want some time to myself," she said.

1. Why does Bechtel prefer to go out for lunch?

   A. To catch up with her work.

   B. To have some time on her own.

TEST 7 詳解

【2019 高考天津卷】

***When** learning to read*, we start off *with sentences, then paragraphs, **and** then stories.* It seemed an unending journey, ***but** as a little girl* I realized knowing how to read could open many doors. My progress *in reading* raised my curiosity. I *often* told my mom to drive *slowly **so that** I could read all the road signs we passed.*

（受詞：knowing how to read；主詞）

　　學習閱讀時，我們從句子開始，然後段落，然後整個故事。這似乎是個永無止盡的旅程，但是從我還是個小女孩時，我就了解到，懂得如何閱讀可以開啓許多道門。我在閱讀方面的進步，提高了我的好奇心。我經常告訴媽媽開車開慢一點，這樣我才能讀到我們經過的所有標誌。

* ***start off*** 著手　　paragraph〔ˈpærəˌgræf〕*n.* 段落
  unending〔ʌnˈɛndɪŋ〕*adj.* 無止盡的
  journey〔ˈdʒɝnɪ〕*n.* 旅行；旅程
  realize〔ˈriəˌlaɪz〕*v.* 了解；理解
  progress〔ˈprɑgrɛs〕*n.* 進步；進展　　raise〔rez〕*v.* 提高
  curiosity〔ˌkjʊrɪˈɑsətɪ〕*n.* 好奇心　　***so that*** 爲了；以便
  sign〔saɪn〕*n.* 記號；符號；標誌；告示
  pass〔pæs〕*v.* 通過

1. (**B**) According to the paragraph, the author's reading of road signs indicates

根據這個段落，作者閱讀道路標誌顯示

(A) her unique way to locate herself.

她指出自己位置的獨特方式。

(B) her eagerness to develop her reading ability.

她想發展閱讀能力的渴望。

* author〔ˈɔθɚ〕*n.* 作者　　reading〔ˈridɪŋ〕*n.* 閱讀

indicate〔ˈɪndəˌket〕*v.* 指示；顯示

unique〔juˈnik〕*adj.* 獨特的

locate〔ˈloket〕*v.* 指出～的位置

eagerness〔ˈigɚnɪs〕*n.* 渴望

develop〔dɪˈvɛləp〕*v.* 發展

ability〔əˈbɪlətɪ〕*n.* 能力

TEST 8 詳解

【2019 高考全國卷】

Marian Bechtel sits *by herself, quietly reading her e-book as she waits for her salad.* Lunch *outside the office* is her "me" time. She works *through lunch at her desk very often.* A lunchtime escape prevents her boss *from interrupting her.*

She returns to work *feeling energized*. "I prefer to be out

alone. I *just* want some time *to myself*," she said.

　　瑪麗安・貝克托獨自坐著，安靜地讀著她的電子書，一邊等候她的
沙拉。午餐是她的「自我」時間。她經常在座位上，一邊工作一邊吃午
餐。午餐時間逃離辦公室，能避免老闆打擾她，她回去上班時就會覺得
精力充沛。「我比較喜歡自己出去。我就是想有些自己的時間，」她如
此說道。

> * Marian Bechtel〔ˈmɛrɪənˈbɛktḷ〕*n.* 瑪麗安・貝克托
> *by oneself* 獨自地；獨力地；靠自己
> quietly〔ˈkwaɪətlɪ〕*adv.* 安靜地　　e-book〔ˈiˌbuk〕*n.* 電子書
> salad〔ˈsæləd〕*n.* 沙拉　　through〔θru〕*prep.* 整個…當中
> lunchtime〔ˈlʌntʃˌtaɪm〕*n.* 午餐時間
> escape〔əˈskep〕*n.* 逃脫；逃離
> prevent〔prɪˈvɛnt〕*v.* 阻止；避免　　boss〔bɔs〕*n.* 老闆
> interrupt〔ˌɪntəˈrʌpt〕*v.* 打斷；中斷　　return〔rɪˈtɜn〕*v.* 返回
> energized〔ˈɛnəˌdʒaɪzd〕*adj.* 充滿活力的（= *energetic*）
> prefer〔prɪˈfɜ〕*v.* 比較喜歡　　out〔aut〕*adv.* 外出
> alone〔əˈlon〕*adj.* 獨自的；單獨的　　*some time* 一些時間
> *to oneself* 只給自己

1. (**B**) Why does Bechtel prefer to go out for lunch?
　　為什麼貝克托比較喜歡出去吃午餐？
　　(A) To catch up with her work. 為了趕上她的工作。
　　(B) To have some time on her own.
　　　　 <u>為了有一些她自己的時間。</u>

> * *go out* 外出　　*catch up with* 追上；趕上
> *on one's own* 靠自己；自己的

TEST 9

【2019 高考北京卷】

Moore spent two years doing research online and trying hard to make a recipe that was both tasty and tooth-friendly. She also asked dentists about teeth cleaning. Finally, she succeeded in making a kind of candy using only natural sweeteners which can reduce oral bacteria. Afterwards, a supermarket agreed to sell Moore's product, and her candy's success began to grow.

1. What does the passage mainly describe?
   A. The way Moore developed her candy.
   B. Where Moore sells her candy.

TEST 10

【 2019 高考浙江卷 】

The loss of big trees was greatest where trees had suffered the greatest water shortage. And the biggest factors increasing water stress have been rising temperatures, which cause trees to lose more water to the air, and early snowmelt, which reduces the water supply available to trees during the dry season.

1. What is a major cause of the water shortage?

   A. A longer dry season.

   B. A warmer climate.

TEST 9 詳解

【2019 高考北京卷】

Moore spent two years *doing research online **and***

*trying hard to make a recipe **that** was both tasty and*

tooth-friendly. She *also* asked dentists *about teeth cleaning.*

Finally, she succeeded in making a kind of candy *using only*

*natural sweeteners **which** can reduce oral bacteria.*

Afterwards, a supermarket agreed to sell Moore's product,

and her candy's success began to grow.

　　摩爾花了兩年的時間在網路上做研究，努力做出又美味又對牙齒好的配方。她也詢問牙醫關於潔牙的事。最後，她成功做出一種糖果，只使用天然的甘味劑，能減少口腔中的細菌。之後，一家超市同意販賣摩爾的產品，她的糖果開始成功。

> * research〔'risɜtʃ〕*n.* 研究　　online〔'ɑn,laɪn〕*adv.* 在網路上
> recipe〔'rɛsəpɪ〕*n.* 調製法　　tasty〔'testɪ〕*adj.* 美味的
> tooth-friendly〔'tuθ,frɛndlɪ〕*adj.* 對牙齒好的
> dentist〔'dɛntɪst〕*n.* 牙醫　　cleaning〔'klinɪŋ〕*n.* 清洗
> succeed〔sək'sid〕*v.* 成功　　kind〔kaɪnd〕*n.* 種類
> natural〔'nætʃərəl〕*adj.* 自然的
> sweetener〔'switn̩ə〕*n.*（人工）甘味料

reduce〔rɪˈdjus〕*v.* 減少　　oral〔ˈorəl〕*adj.* 口部的
bacteria〔bækˈtɪrɪə〕*n. pl.* 細菌
afterwards〔ˈæftɚwɚdz〕*adv.* 之後；後來
supermarket〔ˈsupɚˏmɑrkɪt〕*n.* 超市
agree〔əˈgri〕*v.* 同意　　product〔ˈprɑdəkt〕*n.* 產品
success〔səkˈsɛs〕*n.* 成功

1. (**A**) What does the passage mainly describe?
　　　　這篇短文主要描述什麼？

　　　(A) The way Moore developed her candy.
　　　　 <u>摩爾發展她的糖果的方法。</u>

　　　(B) Where Moore sells her candy.　摩爾賣糖果的地方。

　　　* passage〔ˈpæsɪdʒ〕*n.* 一段（文章）
　　　　mainly〔ˈmenlɪ〕*adv.* 主要地
　　　　describe〔dɪˈskraɪb〕*v.* 描述
　　　　develop〔dɪˈvɛləp〕*v.* 發展；研發

TEST 10 詳解

【 2019 高考浙江卷 】

The loss of big trees was greatest *where trees had*

suffered the greatest water shortage. And the biggest factors

increasing water stress have been rising temperatures, *which* *cause trees to lose more water to the air, **and** early snowmelt,*

which *reduces the water supply available to trees during the*

dry season.

樹木缺水最嚴重的地方，大樹損失最大。用水壓力的增加，最大的因素是逐漸升高的溫度，這會使樹木散失更多水分在空氣中，以及提早融化的雪，這會減少在乾季期間，樹木能夠獲得的供水量。

* loss〔lɔs〕*n.* 損失；損害　　suffer〔'sʌfɚ〕*v.* 遭受；蒙受
　shortage〔'ʃɔrtɪdʒ〕*n.* 短缺；不足
　factor〔'fæktɚ〕*n.* 因素　　increase〔ɪn'kris〕*v.* 增加
　stress〔strɛs〕*n.* 壓力　　rising〔'raɪzɪŋ〕*adj.* 逐漸升高的
　temperature〔'tɛmpərətʃɚ〕*n.* 溫度
　cause〔kɔz〕*v.* 造成　*n.* 原因　　lose〔lus〕*v.* 失去
　snowmelt〔'sno,mɛlt〕*n.* 融雪　　reduce〔rɪ'djus〕*v.* 減少
　supply〔sə'plaɪ〕*n.* 供應；供給
　available〔ə'veləbḷ〕*adj.* 可獲得的；可得到的
　during〔'durɪŋ〕*adv.* 在…的期間
　dry〔draɪ〕*adj.* 乾旱的　　season〔'sizṇ〕*n.* 季；季節

1.(**B**) What is a major cause of the water shortage?
　　缺水主要的原因之一是什麼？

　　(A) A longer dry season. 較長的乾季。

　　(B) A warmer climate. 較溫暖的氣候。

　　* major〔'medʒɚ〕*adj.* 主要的
　　　warm〔wɔrm〕*adj.* 溫暖的
　　　climate〔'klaɪmɪt〕*n.* 氣候

TEST 11

【2019 高考全國卷】

Protecting one's online identity is expensive, but researchers have come up with a low-cost device that keeps others out of private e-space: a smart keyboard that can analyze things like the force of a user's typing and the time between key presses. These patterns are unique to each person. Thus, the keyboard can determine people's identities.

1. Why did the researchers develop the smart keyboard?

A. To reduce pressure on keys.

B. To cut the cost of e-space protection.

TEST 12

【2019 高考全國卷】

During the rosy years of elementary school, I enjoyed sharing, which kept my social status high and made me queen of the playground. Then came my teens. Mean girls and cool kids rose in the ranks not by being friendly but by smoking, breaking rules and playing jokes on others, among whom I soon found myself.

1. What sort of girl was the author in her early years of elementary school?
   A. Unkind.
   B. Generous.

TEST 11 詳解

【 2019 高考全國卷 】

Protecting one's online identity is expensive, **but**

researchers have come up with a low-cost device **that** keeps

others out of private e-space: a smart keyboard **that** can

analyze things like the force of a user's typing **and** the time

between key presses. These patterns are unique *to each*

person. *Thus*, the keyboard can determine people's identities.

保護一個人網路上的身分很昂貴，但是研究人員已經想出了一個低成本的裝置，可以使其他人遠離私人的電子空間：一個智慧型鍵盤，它可以分析像是使用者打字的力道，和按每個鍵的間隔時間等。這些模式每個人都不同，因此，這個鍵盤可以判定人們的身分。

* protect〔prəˋtɛkt〕v. 保護　　online〔ˋɑnˏlaɪn〕adj. 網路上的
  identity〔aɪˋdɛntətɪ〕n. 身分
  researcher〔rɪˋsɝtʃɚ〕n. 研究人員　　**come up with** 想出
  low-cost〔loˋkɔst〕adj. 低成本的　　device〔dɪˋvaɪs〕n. 裝置
  out of 離開　　private〔ˋpraɪvɪt〕adj. 私人的；個人的
  e-space〔ˋiˏspes〕n. 電子空間　　smart〔smɑrt〕adj. 聰明的
  keyboard〔ˋkiˏbord〕n. 鍵盤　　analyze〔ˋænlˏaɪz〕v. 分析
  force〔fors〕n. 力量；強度　　user〔ˋjuzɚ〕n. 使用者
  typing〔ˋtaɪpɪŋ〕n. 打字　　key〔ki〕n.（電腦的）鍵
  press〔prɛs〕n. 壓；按　　pattern〔ˋpætən〕n. 模式

unique〔ju'nik〕*adj.* 獨特的　　thus〔ðʌs〕*adv.* 因此；所以
determine〔dɪ'tɜmɪn〕*v.* 決定；判定

1. (**B**) Why did the researchers develop the smart keyboard?
為什麼研究人員要研發這種聰明的鍵盤？

(A) To reduce pressure on keys.
為了減少在按鍵上的壓力。

(B) To cut the cost of e-space protection.
為了減少保護電子空間的成本。

* develop〔dɪ'vɛləp〕*v.* 發展；研發
reduce〔rɪ'djus〕*v.* 減少　　pressure〔'prɛʃɚ〕*n.* 壓力
cost〔kɔst〕*n.* 費用；成本
protection〔prə'tɛkʃən〕*n.* 保護

TEST 12 詳解

【2019 高考全國卷】

During the rosy years *of elementary school*, I enjoyed

sharing, **which** *kept my social status high* **and** *made me queen*

of the playground. *Then* came my teens. Mean girls and cool

kids rose *in the ranks* **not** *by being friendly* **but** *by smoking,*

breaking rules **and** *playing jokes on others,* *among* **whom** *I*

soon found myself.

　　在小學美好的幾年中，我很喜歡分享，那使我保持高社會地位，成為遊樂場上的女王。接著進入我的青少年時期。惡劣的女孩和冷淡的男孩出頭，他們靠的不是友善，而是吸煙、違規，和對別人惡作劇，很快地，我發現自己也成為他們其中之一。

　　* during〔'dʊrɪŋ〕*prep.* 在⋯期間
　　rosy〔'rozɪ〕*adj.* 玫瑰色的；美好的；光明的
　　elementary〔ˌɛlə'mɛntərɪ〕*adj.* 初等的；基本的
　　elementary school 小學　　enjoy〔ɪn'dʒɔɪ〕*v.* 喜歡
　　share〔ʃɛr〕*v.* 分享　　social〔'soʃəl〕*adj.* 社會的
　　status〔'stetəs〕*n.* 地位　　queen〔kwin〕*n.* 女王
　　playground〔'pleˌɡraʊnd〕*n.* 運動場；遊樂場
　　teens〔tinz〕*n.* 十幾歲的年齡
　　mean〔min〕*adj.* 卑鄙的；惡劣的
　　cool〔kul〕*adj.* 冷淡的；不友善的　　kid〔kɪd〕*n.* 小孩
　　rise〔raɪz〕*v.* 出頭；升起　　rank〔ræŋk〕*n.* 地位；階級
　　not A but B 不是 A 而是 B　　rule〔rul〕*n.* 規則；規定
　　break a rule 違反規則　　joke〔dʒok〕*n.* 笑話；惡作劇
　　play a joke on sb. 作弄某人；對某人惡作劇
　　among〔ə'mʌŋ〕*prep.* 在⋯之中

1. (**B**) What sort of girl was the author in her early years of
　　 elementary school? 作者在她小學初期是怎樣的女孩？
　　 (A) Unkind. 不親切的。
　　 (B) Generous. <u>慷慨的。</u>

　　 * sort〔sɔrt〕*n.* 種類　　author〔'ɔθɚ〕*n.* 作者
　　 unkind〔ʌn'kaɪnd〕*adj.* 不親切的；無情的
　　 generous〔'dʒɛnərəs〕*adj.* 慷慨的

TEST 13

【2019 高考全國卷】

Before the 1830s, most newspapers in America were sold through annual subscriptions, usually $8 to $10 a year. Back then, these amounts were unaffordable for most citizens. Accordingly, newspapers were read almost solely by rich people. Besides, few newspapers appealed to a mass audience. They were dull and visually unpleasant. But a revolution in the 1830s changed all that.

1. Which of the following best describes newspapers in America before the 1830s?
   A. Unattractive.
   B. Inexpensive.

TEST 14

【2019 高考天津卷】

Most of my reading through primary, middle and high school was factual reading. I read for knowledge, and to make A's on my tests. Occasionally, I would read a novel that was assigned, but I didn't enjoy this type of reading. I liked facts, things that are concrete. I thought anything abstract left too much room for argument.

1. What was the author's view on factual reading?

　A. It would help her improve her test scores.

　B. It would allow much room for free thinking.

TEST 13 詳解

【2019 高考全國卷】

Before the 1830s, most newspapers *in America* were sold *through annual subscriptions, usually $8 to $10 a year. Back then*, these amounts were unaffordable *for most citizens. Accordingly*, newspapers were read *almost solely by rich people. Besides*, few newspapers appealed to a mass audience. They were dull **and** *visually* unpleasant. **But** a revolution *in the 1830s* changed all that.

在 1830 年代以前，美國的報紙銷售都是透過年度訂閱，通常一年要 8 到 10 美元。在那時，這些金額是大部分人民負擔不起的。因此，報紙幾乎都只有有錢人在讀。此外，很少有報紙會吸引廣大的讀者，因為內容無聊，視覺上也不好看。但是，1830 年代的大變革改變了這一切。

* through〔θru〕*adv.* 從頭到尾
  annual〔'ænjʊəl〕*adj.* 每年的；年度的
  subscription〔səb'skrɪpʃən〕*n.* 訂閱
  amount〔ə'maʊnt〕*n.* 數量
  unaffordable〔ˌʌnə'fordəbḷ〕*adj.* 負擔不起的
  citizen〔'sɪtəzn̩〕*n.* 公民；國民
  accordingly〔ə'kɔrdɪŋlɪ〕*adv.* 因此；所以
  solely〔'sollɪ〕*adv.* 單獨；獨自

appeal〔əˋpil〕 v. 吸引 < to >　　 mass〔mæs〕 adj. 大量的

audience〔ˋɔdɪəns〕 n. 觀眾；聽眾

dull〔dʌl〕 adj. 無聊的；乏味的

visually〔ˋvɪʒʊəlɪ〕 adv. 視覺上地

unpleasant〔ʌnˋplɛzn̩t〕 adj. 令人不快的

revolution〔͵rɛvəˋluʃən〕 n. 革命；變革

1. (**A**) Which of the following best describes newspapers in America before the 1830s?

下列何者最能描述 1830 年代以前的美國報紙？

(A) Unattractive. 沒有吸引力的。

(B) Inexpensive. 不貴的。

* following〔ˋfɑloɪŋ〕 adj. 以下的

describe〔dɪˋskraɪb〕 v. 描述

unattractive〔͵ʌnəˋtræktɪv〕 adj. 沒有吸引力的

inexpensive〔͵ɪnɪkˋspɛnsɪv〕 adj. 不貴的

TEST 14 詳解

【2019 高考天津卷】

Most of my reading *through primary, middle and high*

school was factual reading.　I read *for knowledge*, **and** *to make*

A's on my tests.　*Occasionally*, I would read a novel **that** *was*

assigned, **but** I didn't enjoy this type of reading.　I liked facts, *things **that** are concrete.* I thought anything *abstract* left too

much room *for argument.*

　　從小學、國中，一直到高中，我大部分的閱讀都是事實閱讀。我閱讀是爲了知識，還有爲了考試考 A。偶爾我也會讀規定的小說，但是我不喜歡這種閱讀。我喜歡事實，具體的事物。我覺得，抽象的事物有太多爭議的空間。

　　　* through〔θru〕*prep.* 在整個～期間
　　　　primary〔'praɪ,mɛrɪ〕*adj.* 初級的
　　　　middle〔'mɪdl̩〕*adj.* 中級的
　　　　factual〔'fæktʃʊəl〕*adj.* 事實的；有關事實的
　　　　knowledge〔'nɑlɪdʒ〕*n.* 知識
　　　　occasionally〔ə'keʒənl̩ɪ〕*adv.* 偶爾；有時
　　　　novel〔'nɑvl̩〕*n.* 小說　　　assign〔ə'saɪn〕*v.* 分配；指定
　　　　type〔taɪp〕*n.* 類型
　　　　concrete〔kɑn'krit , 'kɑnkrit〕*adj.* 具體的
　　　　abstract〔'æbstrækt〕*adj.* 抽象的　　　room〔rum〕*n.* 空間
　　　　argument〔'ɑrgjəmənt〕*n.* 爭論

1. (**A**) What was the author's view on factual reading?
　　　有關事實閱讀，作者的看法爲何？
　　　(A) It would help her improve her test scores.
　　　　它會幫助改善她的考試成績。
　　　(B) It would allow much room for free thinking.
　　　　它會給予很多自由思考的空間。

　　　　* author〔'ɔθɚ〕*n.* 作者　　　view〔vju〕*n.* 想法；見解
　　　　improve〔ɪm'pruv〕*v.* 改善　　　score〔skor〕*n.* 分數；成績
　　　　allow〔ə'lau〕*v.* 允許；給予　　　thinking〔'θɪŋkɪŋ〕*n.* 思考

TEST 15

【2019 高考全國卷】

NASA HUNCH high school classrooms are designed to connect high school classrooms with NASA engineers. "We don't give the students any breaks. They have to do it just like NASA engineers," says the project manager. "There are no tests. There is no graded homework. There almost are no grades, other than 'Are you working toward your goal?'"

1. What is the purpose of the HUNCH program?
   A. To strengthen teacher-student relationships.
   B. To link space technology with school education.

TEST 16

【2018 高考天津卷】

Fire extinguishers are located on each floor and in each apartment. Use one only if you have been trained to do so. Irresponsible use of one can create a dangerous situation and could cause damage to personal property. Misuse of one will result in fines.

1. What do we know about the use of fire extinguishers?
   A. Using one wrongly results in punishment.
   B. Improper use of them can destroy the building.

TEST 15 詳解

【 2019 高考全國卷 】

NASA HUNCH high school classrooms are designed to connect high school classrooms *with NASA engineers.* "We don't give the students any breaks. They have to do it *just like NASA engineers,*" says the project manager. "There are no tests. There is no graded homework. There *almost* are no grades, **other than** '*Are you working toward your goal?*'"

　　NASA HUNCH 高中敎室的設計，是將高中敎室和 NASA 的工程師連結在一起。「我們不會給學生任何休息時間。他們做事必須像 NASA 的工程師一樣，」計畫經理說道。「這個計畫沒有考試，沒有要打分數的作業，也幾乎沒有成績，除了『你正在朝你的目標前進嗎？』」

* NASA〔'næsə〕*n.*（美國）航空及太空總署（ = *National Aeronautics and Space Administration* ）
hunch〔hʌntʃ〕*n.* 預感；直覺　　design〔dɪ'zaɪn〕*v.* 設計
connect〔kə'nɛkt〕*v.* 連接；結合
engineer〔ˌɛndʒə'nɪr〕*n.* 工程師
break〔brek〕*n.* 休息時間　　project〔'prɑdʒɛkt〕*n.* 計畫
manager〔'mænɪdʒɚ〕*n.* 經理
grade〔gred〕*v.* 評分；打分數　　*n.* 分數；成績
homework〔'hom,wɝk〕*n.* 家庭作業

almost〔'ɔl,most〕*adv.* 幾乎　　***other than*** 除了
toward〔tord〕*prep.* 朝向…　　goal〔gol〕*n.* 目標

1. (**B**) What is the purpose of the HUNCH program?
這個 HUNCH 計畫的目的是什麼？

(A) To strengthen teacher-student relationships.
加強師生關係。

(B) To link space technology with school education.
<u>連結太空科技和學校教育。</u>

* purpose〔'pɝpəs〕*n.* 目的　　program〔'progræm〕*n.* 計畫
strengthen〔'strɛŋ(k)θən〕*v.* 加強
relationship〔rɪ'leʃən,ʃɪp〕*n.* 關係
link〔lɪŋk〕*v.* 連接；結合　　space〔spes〕*n.* 太空
technology〔tɛk'nɑlədʒɪ〕*n.* 科技
education〔,ɛdʒə'keʃən〕*n.* 教育

TEST 16 詳解

【2018 高考天津卷】

Fire extinguishers are located *on each floor **and** in each apartment.* Use one *only **if** you have been trained to do so.* Irresponsible use *of one* can create a dangerous situation ***and*** could cause damage *to personal property.* Misuse *of one* will result in fines.

　　每一層樓和每一間公寓裡都配置有滅火器。唯有受過訓練，方可使用。不負責任任意使用，可能會產生很危險的情況，可能對個人財產造成損害。誤用者會處以罰款。

* extinguisher〔ɪkˋstɪŋgwɪʃə〕 *n.* 滅火器
fire extinguisher 滅火器　　locate〔loˋket , ˋloket〕 *v.* 設置
floor〔flor〕 *n.* 地板；樓層
apartment〔əˋpartmənt〕 *n.* 公寓　　train〔tren〕 *v.* 訓練
irresponsible〔͵ɪrɪˋspansəbḷ〕 *adj.* 不負責任的
create〔krɪˋet〕 *v.* 創造；製造
dangerous〔ˋdendʒərəs〕 *adj.* 危險的
situation〔͵sɪtʃʊˋeʃən〕 *n.* 情形　　cause〔kɔz〕 *v.* 造成；導致
damage〔ˋdæmɪdʒ〕 *n.* 損害；損失
personal〔ˋpɝsṇl〕 *adj.* 個人的；私人的
property〔ˋprapətɪ〕 *n.* 財產；資產
misuse〔mɪsˋjus〕 *n.* 誤用；濫用 < *of* >
result in 導致；造成 (= *cause*)
fine〔faɪn〕 *n.* 罰金；罰款

1. (**A**) What do we know about the use of fire extinguishers?
關於滅火器的使用，我們知道什麼？
(A) Using one wrongly results in punishment.
<u>不當使用會導致處罰。</u>
(B) Improper use of them can destroy the building.
不當的使用會毀掉建築物。

* wrongly〔ˋrɔŋlɪ〕 *adv.* 錯誤地；不當地
punishment〔ˋpʌnɪʃmənt〕 *n.* 處罰；刑罰
improper〔ɪmˋprapə〕 *adj.* 錯誤的；不當的
destroy〔dɪˋstrɔɪ〕 *v.* 破壞；毀壞

TEST 17

【2018 高考天津卷】

There's a new frontier in 3D printing: food. Recent developments have made 3D food printers possible. Making complicated chocolate sculptures normally requires years of experience, but a printer makes it easy. A restaurant in Spain uses a Foodini to "re-create" food that is "exactly the same," freeing cooks to complete other tasks. In another restaurant, all of the dishes and desserts it serves are 3D-printed.

1. What benefit does 3D printing bring to food production?

   A. It saves time and effort in cooking.

   B. It improves the cooking conditions.

TEST 17 詳解

【2018 高考天津卷】

There's a new frontier *in 3D printing*: food. Recent

developments have made <u>3D food printers</u> *possible*. Making
　　　　　　　　V.　　　　　O.　　　　　OC.

complicated chocolate sculptures *normally* requires years of
────── 動名詞做主詞 ──────

experience, ***but*** a printer makes it *easy*. A restaurant *in Spain*
　　　　　　　　　　　　V.　　O. OC.

uses a Foodini to "re-create" food ***that*** is *"exactly the same,"*

freeing cooks to complete other tasks. In another restaurant,

all of the dishes and desserts *it serves* are 3D-printed.

　　3D 列印有了一個新領域：食品。近來的發展造就了 3D 食品列印的
可能性。製作複雜的巧克力雕刻，通常需要數年的經驗，但是有了 3D
食品列印機就容易了。西班牙一家餐廳，使用一台 Foodini 食品列印機
【這個名字源自 Houdini，史上最有名的魔術師胡迪尼】，可以複製出完全
一樣的食物，讓廚師們有時間去完成其他工作。還有另一家餐廳，他們
供應的所有餐點和甜點，都是用 3D 列印出來的。

　　* frontier〔frʌnˈtɪr〕*n.* 最前端；未開拓的領域
　　　printing〔ˈprɪntɪŋ〕*n.* 印刷；列印
　　　recent〔ˈrisn̩t〕*adj.* 最近的

development〔dɪˈvɛləpmənt〕*n.* 發展

printer〔ˈprɪntɚ〕*n.* 印表機

complicated〔ˈkɑmpləˌketɪd〕*adj.* 複雜的

chocolate〔ˈtʃɔklɪt〕*n.* 巧克力

sculpture〔ˈskʌlptʃɚ〕*n.* 雕刻

normally〔ˈnɔrml̩ɪ〕*adv.* 通常

require〔rɪˈkwaɪr〕*v.* 要求;需要

experience〔ɪkˈspɪrɪəns〕*n.* 經驗

Spain〔spen〕*n.* 西班牙

Foodini, a 3D food printer

re-create〔ˌrikrɪˈet〕*v.* 重新創造;再做

exactly〔ɪgˈzæktlɪ〕*adv.* 正確地;精確地

free〔fri〕*v.* 使自由;解放　　cook〔kʊk〕*n.* 廚師

complete〔kəmˈplit〕*v.* 完成

task〔tæsk〕*n.* 任務;工作　　dish〔dɪʃ〕*n.* 菜餚

dessert〔dɪˈzɜt〕*n.* 甜點　　serve〔sɜv〕*v.* 供應

1. (**A**) What benefit does 3D printing bring to food production?

   3D 列印爲食物製造帶來什麼好處?

   (A) It saves time and effort in cooking.

   　　它在烹調上節省時間和努力。

   (B) It improves the cooking conditions.

   　　它改善烹調的條件。

   * benefit〔ˈbɛnəfɪt〕*n.* 利益;好處

   　production〔prəˈdʌkʃən〕*n.* 製造;生產

   　save〔sev〕*v.* 節省　　effort〔ˈɛfɚt〕*n.* 努力

   　cooking〔ˈkʊkɪŋ〕*n.* 烹調

   　improve〔ɪmˈpruv〕*v.* 改善

   　condition〔kənˈdɪʃən〕*n.* 狀況;條件

TEST 18

【2018 高考天津卷】

Most of us observed much more as children than we do as adults. A child's day is filled with fascination, newness and wonder. Curiosity gave us all a natural awareness. But as we grow older, we become numb to new stimulation and new ideas.

1. According to the paragraph, compared with adults, children are more _____.

    A. anxious to do wonders

    B. eager to explore the world around them

TEST 19

【 2018 高考天津卷 】

The obsession many have with naming things blocks awareness. I have seen bird watchers who spotted a bird, immediately looked it up in a field guide, and said, a "ruby-crowned kinglet" and checked it off. They no longer paid attention to the bird and never learned what it was doing.

1. The bird watchers' behavior shows that they _____.

   A. care only about the names of birds

   B. question the accuracy of the field guides

TEST 18 詳解

【2018 高考天津卷】

Most of us observed much more *as children **than** we do*

as adults. A child's day is filled *with fascination, newness*

and wonder. Curiosity gave us all a natural awareness. *But*

as** we grow older*, we become numb *to new stimulation **and

new ideas.

　　我們大部分的人，小時候所觀察到的事物，比我們長大成年時多更多。童年的日子裡，充滿了令人著迷的事物，新奇和驚嘆。好奇心給予我們所有人對大自然的意識。但是，隨著我們日漸年長，我們對於新的刺激和新的想法變得麻木。

* observe〔əb'zɜv〕v. 觀察　　adult〔ə'dʌlt〕n. 成年人
be filled with 充滿　　fascination〔ˌfæsn̩'eʃən〕n. 著迷；魅力
newness〔'nunɪs〕n. 新奇；新發現
wonder〔'wʌndə〕n. 驚奇；驚嘆
curiosity〔ˌkjʊrɪ'ɑsətɪ〕n. 好奇心
natural〔'nætʃərəl〕adj. 自然的
awareness〔ə'wɛrnɪs〕n. 察覺；意識
numb〔nʌm〕adj. 麻木的；無感覺的
stimulation〔ˌstɪmjə'leʃən〕n. 刺激
idea〔aɪ'diə〕n. 主意；構想

1.(**B**) According to the paragraph, compared with adults, children are more _____.

根據這個段落，和成年人比起來，小孩比較 _____。

(A) anxious to do wonders 渴望做出驚人的成就

(B) eager to explore the world around them
    渴望去探索他們周遭的世界

* paragraph〔ˈpærəˌgræf〕*n.* 段落
  compare〔kəmˈpɛr〕*v.* 比較　　***compared with*** 和~比較
  anxious〔ˈæŋkʃəs〕*adj.* 焦慮的；渴望的
  do wonders 創造奇蹟；做出驚人的成就
  eager〔ˈigɚ〕*adj.* 渴望的
  explore〔ɪkˈsplor〕*v.* 探險；探索

TEST 19 詳解

【2018 高考天津卷】

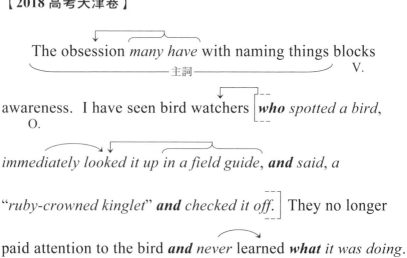

The obsession *many have* with naming things blocks
────────── 主詞 ──────────　　　　　V.

awareness. I have seen bird watchers ⎡*who* spotted a bird,
O.

immediately looked it up in a field guide, ***and*** *said*, a

"*ruby-crowned kinglet*" ***and*** *checked it off.*⎤ They no longer

paid attention to the bird ***and*** *never* learned ***what*** *it was doing.*

　　許多人對於事物命名的執念，會阻礙他們的意識。我曾經見過賞鳥人看到了一隻鳥、立刻查閱野外指南，說著「紅頂戴菊鳥」，然後打了個勾。他們再也不注意那隻鳥，也從來都不知道它在做什麼。

* obsession〔əbˋsɛʃən〕*n.* 著迷；妄想；執念
  name〔nem〕*v.* 命名　　block〔blɑk〕*v.* 阻擋；阻礙
  awareness〔əˋwɛrnɪs〕*n.* 察覺；意識
  watcher〔ˋwɑtʃɚ〕*n.* 觀賞者　　spot〔spɑt〕*v.* 發現
  immediately〔ɪˋmidɪɪtlɪ〕*adv.* 立刻；直接地
  look up 查閱　　field〔fild〕*n.* 原野；野外
  guide〔gaɪd〕*n.* 導遊；指南　　***field guide*** 野外指南
  ruby-crowned〔ˋrubɪˏkraʊnd〕*adj.* 頭頂有鮮紅色的
  kinglet〔ˋkɪŋlɪt〕*n.* 戴菊鳥
  check off 在…上打勾表示已核對
  no longer 不再　　***pay attention to*** 注意

1. (**A**) The bird watchers' behavior shows that they _____.
   這些賞鳥者的行為顯示出他們 _____。

   (A) care only about the names of birds
   　　只在意鳥類的名字

   (B) question the accuracy of the field guides
   　　質疑野外指南的正確度

   * behavior〔bɪˋhevjɚ〕*n.* 行為；舉止
     show〔ʃo〕*v.* 顯示
     care〔kɛr〕*v.* 在意；關心
     accuracy〔ˋækjərəsɪ〕*n.* 正確性；準確性

TEST 20

【 2018 高考天津卷 】

With global population growth, food production needs to be raised considerably. 3D food printing could contribute to solving this problem. Some experts believe printers could use materials from plentiful renewable resources like algae and grass to replace traditional ingredients. 3D printing can also reduce fuel use and emissions. Future "food" may last years, reducing transportation and storage requirements.

1. What can we learn about 3D food printing from the paragraph?

   A. It needs no space for the storage of food.

   B. It could use renewable materials as sources of food.

TEST 20 詳解

【 2018 高考天津卷 】

With global population growth, food production needs

to be raised *considerably*. 3D food printing could contribute

to solving this problem. Some experts believe printers could

use materials *from plentiful renewable resources like algae*

and grass to replace traditional ingredients. 3D printing can

also reduce fuel use and emissions. Future "food" may last

years, *reducing transportation **and** storage requirements.*

　　隨著全球人口的成長，食物的產量必須大幅提升。3D 食品列印或許有助於解決這個問題。有一些專家相信，3D 食品列印可以使用豐富的可再生資源做為原料，像海藻和草等，以取代傳統原料。3D 列印可以減少燃料的使用和排放。未來的「食物」可能可以持續數年不腐壞，減少運輸和貯藏的必要條件。

　　* global〔ˋglobḷ〕*adj.* 全球的
　　population〔͵pɑpjəˋleʃən〕*n.* 人口　　growth〔groθ〕*n.* 成長
　　production〔prəˋdʌkʃən〕*n.* 生產；產量
　　raise〔rez〕*v.* 提高；增加
　　considerably〔kənˋsɪdərəbḷɪ〕*adv.* 大幅地
　　contribute〔kənˋtrɪbjut〕*v.* 提供；貢獻

contribute to 促成；有助於　　solve〔sɑlv〕*v.* 解決
expert〔'ɛkspɜt〕*n.* 專家　　printer〔'prɪntɚ〕*n.* 印表機
material〔mə'tɪrɪəl〕*n.* 材料；原料
plentiful〔'plɛntɪfəl〕*adj.* 很多的；豐富的
renewable〔rɪ'nuəbḷ〕*adj.* 可更新的；可再生的
resource〔rɪ'sors〕*n.* 資源　　algae〔'ældʒi〕*n. pl.* 海藻
grass〔græs〕*n.* 草　　replace〔rɪ'ples〕*v.* 取代
traditional〔trə'dɪʃənḷ〕*adj.* 傳統的
ingredient〔ɪn'gridɪənt〕*n.* 成分；原料
reduce〔rɪ'djus〕*v.* 減少　　fuel〔'fjuəl〕*n.* 燃料
emission〔ɪ'mɪʃən〕*n.* 排放（物、量）
future〔'fjutʃɚ〕*n., adj.* 未來（的）
last〔læst〕*v.* 持續；耐久；不腐壞
transportation〔ˌtrænspɚ'teʃən〕*n.* 運輸；輸送
storage〔'storɪdʒ〕*n.* 貯藏；儲存
requirement〔rɪ'kwaɪrmənt〕*n.* 必要條件

1. (**B**) What can we learn about 3D food printing from the
paragraph?
關於 3D 食品列印，從這個段落我們可以得知什麼？

(A) It needs no space for the storage of food.
它不需要空間來貯藏食物。

(B) It could use renewable materials as sources of food.
<u>它可使用可再生材料來當做食物的來源。</u>

* learn〔lɜn〕*v.* 得知　　paragraph〔'pærəˌgræf〕*n.* 段落
space〔spes〕*n.* 空間　　source〔sors〕*n.* 來源

TEST 21

【2018 高考天津卷】

If you have a smoke detector installed in your apartment, please do the following to ensure its safe operation.

----If it is working properly, the red light should be on. If the red light is not blinking, contact your landlord immediately.

----Do not cover or block it in any way.

----If an alarm goes off but there is no fire or smoke, inform a specialist.

1. To ensure the safe operation of a smoke detector, one should _____.

　A.　contact a specialist regularly

　B.　make certain the red light is working

TEST 21 詳解

【2018 高考天津卷】

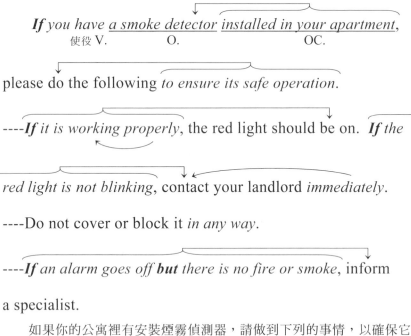

If you have <u>a smoke detector</u> <u>installed in your apartment</u>,
使役 V.　　　　　　O.　　　　　　　OC.

please do the following *to ensure its safe operation.*

----*If it is working properly*, the red light should be on. *If the*

red light is not blinking, contact your landlord *immediately.*

----Do not cover or block it *in any way.*

----*If an alarm goes off **but** there is no fire or smoke*, inform

a specialist.

　　如果你的公寓裡有安裝煙霧偵測器，請做到下列的事情，以確保它的安全運轉。
----如果運作正常的話，紅燈應該會亮著。如果紅燈沒有在閃，請立即聯絡你的房東。
----偵測器上絕不可覆蓋或擋到東西。
----如果警報響了，但沒有火也沒有煙霧，請通知專人。

　　　* smoke〔smok〕*n.* 煙　　detector〔dɪˈtɛktə〕*n.* 偵測器
　　　install〔ɪnˈstɔl〕*v.* 安裝　　apartment〔əˈpartmənt〕*n.* 公寓
　　　the following 下列的事
　　　ensure〔ɪnˈʃur〕*v.* 保證；確保　　safe〔sef〕*adj.* 安全的

operation〔͵ɑpə'reʃən〕*n.* 操作；運轉

work〔wɜk〕*v.* 運作

properly〔'prɑpə-lɪ〕*adv.* 適當地；正確地

on〔ɑn〕*prep.* (燈) 開著的

blink〔blɪŋk〕*v.* 忽明忽滅；閃爍

contact〔'kɑntækt〕*v.* 聯絡；聯繫

landlord〔'lænd͵lɔrd〕*n.* 房東

immediately〔ɪ'midɪɪtlɪ〕*adv.* 立即；立刻

cover〔'kʌvə-〕*v.* 覆蓋　　block〔blɑk〕*v.* 阻擋

not⋯in any way 絕不 (= *not⋯at all*)

alarm〔ə'lɑrm〕*n.* 警報器　　***go off*** 鳴響

fire〔faɪr〕*n.* 火　　inform〔ɪn'fɔrm〕*v.* 通知；告知

specialist〔'spɛʃəlɪst〕*n.* 專家

1. (**B**) To ensure the safe operation of a smoke detector,
one should _____.

為了確保煙霧偵測器安全運轉，我們應該 _____。

(A) contact a specialist regularly
定期聯絡專家

(B) make certain the red light is working
確定紅燈在閃

* regularly〔'rɛgjələ-lɪ〕*adv.* 定期地

certain〔'sɜtṇ〕*adj.* 確定的 (= *sure*)

make certain 確定 (= *make sure*)

TEST 22

【2018 高考北京卷】

At Space Camp, trainees can earn their Space Exploration badge by building and firing model rockets, learning about space tasks and trying simulated flying to space with a crew from all over the world.

1. To earn a Space Exploration badge, a trainee needs to _____.

   A. fly to space

   B. build and fire model rockets

TEST 22 詳解

【 **2018 高考北京卷** 】

At Space Camp, trainees can earn their Space Exploration

badge *by building and firing model rockets, learning about*

*space tasks **and** trying simulated flying to space with a crew*

from all over the world.

　　在太空營裡，學員們組建和發射模型火箭、學習有關太空任務的事情，還有和來自全世界的組員一起，嘗試模擬飛行上太空，就可以獲得太空探索徽章。

* space〔spes〕*n.* 太空　　　camp〔kæmp〕*n.* 營地
　trainee〔tren'i〕*n.* 受訓者；學員　　earn〔ɝn〕*v.* 博得；獲得
　exploration〔͵ɛksplə'reʃən〕*n.* 探險；探索
　badge〔bædʒ〕*n.* 徽章　　fire〔faɪr〕*v.* 發射
　model〔'madḷ〕*adj.* 模型的　　rocket〔'rɑkɪt〕*n.* 火箭
　task〔tæsk〕*n.* 工作；任務
　simulated〔'sɪmjə͵letɪd〕*adj.* 模擬的
　crew〔kru〕*n.* 全體工作人員

1. (**B**) To earn a Space Exploration badge, a trainee needs
　　 to _____.
　　 為了獲得太空探險徽章，學員需要 _____ 。
　　 (A) fly to space. 飛往太空。
　　 (B) build and fire model rockets. 組建和發射模型火箭。

TEST 23

【2018 高考天津卷】

Future 3D food printers could make processed food healthier. Food printing could allow consumers to print food with customized nutritional content, like vitamins. The amount of protein, fat, and sodium could also be controlled.

1. According to the paragraph, 3D-printed food

   A. is more available to consumers.

   B. can meet individual nutritional needs.

TEST 24

【2018 高考天津卷】

To awaken your senses, stop predicting what you are going to see and feel before it occurs. One chilly night when I was hiking with some students, I mentioned we were going to cross a stream. The students began complaining about how cold it would be. We reached the stream, and they unwillingly walked ahead. They were almost knee-deep before they realized it was a hot spring.

1. What idea does the author convey in the paragraph?
   A. One should avoid jumping to conclusions.
   B. One should stop complaining all the time.

TEST 23 詳解

【2018 高考天津卷】

Future 3D food printers could make <u>processed food</u>
　　　　　　　　　　　　　　　 V.　　　 O.

healthier. Food printing could allow consumers to print food
OC.

with customized nutritional content, like vitamins. The amount

of protein, fat, and sodium could *also* be controlled.

未來的 3D 食品列印機，可以讓加工食品更加健康。3D 食品列印可以讓消費者列印出，客製化營養含量的食物，如維他命。蛋白質、脂肪和鈉含量也都可以控制。

* future〔ˈfjutʃɚ〕*n., adj.* 未來（的）
  printer〔ˈprɪntɚ〕*n.* 印表機
  processed〔ˈprɑsɛst〕*adj.* 加工的
  healthy〔ˈhɛlθɪ〕*adj.* 健康的；衛生的
  printing〔ˈprɪntɪŋ〕*n.* 列印　　allow〔əˈlaʊ〕*v.* 允許
  consumer〔kənˈsumɚ〕*n.* 消費者
  customized〔ˈkʌstəˌmaɪzd〕*adj.* 定做的；客製化的
  nutritional〔nuˈtrɪʃənl̩〕*adj.* 營養的
  content〔ˈkɑntɛnt〕*n.* 內容；含量
  vitamin〔ˈvaɪtəmɪn〕*n.* 維他命　　amount〔əˈmaʊnt〕*n.* 數量
  protein〔ˈprotiɪn〕*n.* 蛋白質　　fat〔fæt〕*n.* 脂肪
  sodium〔ˈsodɪəm〕*n.* 鈉　　control〔kənˈtrol〕*v.* 控制

1. (**B**) According to the paragraph, 3D-printed food
根據這個段落，3D 列印的食品

　(A) is more available to consumers.
　　　消費者更加容易得到。

　(B) can meet individual nutritional needs.
　　　<u>可以滿足個別的營養需要。</u>

　* paragraph〔ˋpærəˏgræf〕 *n.* 段落
　　available〔əˋveləbḷ〕 *adj.* 可獲得的
　　meet a need 滿足需求
　　individual〔ˏɪndəˋvɪdʒʊəl〕 *adj.* 個別的

TEST 24 詳解

【2018 高考天津卷】

To awaken your senses, stop predicting ***what* you are**

going to see *and* feel *before* it occurs. *One chilly night **when***

I was hiking with some students, I mentioned we were going

to cross a stream. The students began complaining about

how* cold it would be**. We reached the stream, ***and they

——受詞——

unwillingly walked ahead. They were almost knee-deep

***before* they realized it was a hot spring.**

要激起你的感官,在事情發生之前,不要預測你即將看到或感覺到的。在一個很冷的晚上,當我和一些學生在健行時,我提到我們要過一條小溪,學生們就開始抱怨溪水會有多冷。我們到達溪邊,他們不情願地往前走。走到幾乎水深及膝時,他們才曉得那是個溫泉。

* awaken〔əˋwekən〕v. 喚醒;激起
  sense〔sɛns〕n. 感覺;感官　　predict〔prɪˋdɪkt〕v. 預測
  occur〔əˋkɝ〕v. 發生　　chilly〔ˋtʃɪlɪ〕adj. 寒冷的
  hike〔haɪk〕v. 健行　　mention〔ˋmɛnʃən〕v. 提到
  cross〔krɔs〕v. 橫越;越過　　stream〔strim〕n. 溪流;河流
  complain〔kəmˋplen〕v. 抱怨 < about >
  reach〔ritʃ〕v. 到達;抵達
  unwillingly〔ʌnˋwɪlɪŋlɪ〕adv. 不情願地;不願意地
  ahead〔əˋhɛd〕adv. 向前
  knee-deep〔ˋniˏdip〕adj. 深及膝蓋的
  realize〔ˋriəˏlaɪz〕v. 了解;理解
  spring〔sprɪŋ〕n. 泉水　　*hot spring* 溫泉

1. (**A**) What idea does the author convey in the paragraph?
  在這個段落裡,作者要傳達什麼想法?
  (A) One should avoid jumping to conclusions.
  　　人應該避免草率下結論。
  (B) One should stop complaining all the time.
  　　人應該停止一直抱怨。

  * idea〔aɪˋdiə〕n. 主意;想法　　author〔ˋɔθɚ〕n. 作者
  convey〔kənˋve〕v. 傳達
  paragraph〔ˋpærəˏgræf〕n. 段落
  avoid〔əˋvɔɪd〕v. 避免;逃避
  conclusion〔kənˋkluʒən〕n. 結論
  jump to conclusions 遽下結論;草率下結論
  all the time 經常

TEST 25

【 2018 高考北京卷 】

Humans produce more than 300 million tons of plastic every year. Almost half of that winds up in landfills, and up to 12 million tons pollute the oceans. So far there is no effective way to get rid of it, but a new study suggests an answer may lie in the stomachs of some hungry worms.

1. What can we learn about the worms in the study?

A. They can consume plastics.

B. They wind up in landfills.

TEST 25 詳解

【2018 高考北京卷】

Humans produce more than 300 million tons of plastic *every year*. Almost half of that winds up in landfills, **and** up to 12 million tons pollute the oceans. *So far* there is no effective way *to get rid of it*, **but** a new study suggests an answer may lie in the stomachs *of some hungry worms*.

人們每年製造超過三億噸的塑膠。其中大約一半最後都到了垃圾掩埋場，而高達一千二百萬噸污染了海洋。到目前為止，還沒有有效的方法可以消除，但是一項新的研究顯示，有一個答案可能在於一些飢餓小蟲的胃裡。

* human〔'hjumən〕*n.* 人　　produce〔prə'djus〕*v.* 製造；生產
  ton〔tʌn〕*n.* 噸　　plastic〔'plæstɪk〕*n.* 塑膠
  wind〔waɪnd〕*v.* 纏繞；上發條　　**wind up** 最後；結束
  landfill〔'lændfɪl〕*n.* 垃圾掩埋場　　**up to** 多達；高達
  pollute〔pə'lut〕*v.* 污染　　**so far** 到目前為止
  effective〔ə'fɛktɪv〕*adj.* 有效的　　**get rid of** 消除
  study〔'stʌdɪ〕*n.* 研究　　suggest〔sə(g)'dʒɛst〕*v.* 顯示
  lie in 在於　　worm〔wɜm〕*n.* 蟲

1. (**A**) What can we learn about the worms in the study?
   關於在研究中的蟲我們可以得知什麼？
   (A) They can consume plastics. 牠們可以吃掉塑膠。
   (B) They wind up in landfills. 牠們最後在垃圾掩埋場。
   * learn〔lɜn〕*v.* 得知　　consume〔kən'sum〕*v.* 吃（喝）

TEST 26

【2018 高考天津卷】

3D food printing still has challenges to overcome. Currently, most ingredients must be changed to a paste first, and the printing process is quite time-consuming. Besides, most of the 3D food printers now are restricted to dry ingredients because meat and milk products may easily go bad. Some experts think 3D food printers are better suited for fast food restaurants than homes and high-end restaurants.

1. What is the main factor that prevents 3D food printing from spreading widely?

A. 3D food printers are too expensive.

B. The printing process is long and complicated.

TEST 27

【 2018 高考浙江卷 】

Look at reusable shopping bags. The stronger a reusable bag is, the longer its life and the more plastic-bag use it cancels out. However, longer-lasting reusable bags often require more energy to make. A cotton bag must be used at least 131 times to be better for the planet than plastic.

1. What is a disadvantage of reusable bags?
   A. They are less strong than plastic bags.
   B. Producing them requires more energy.

TEST 26 詳解

【2018 高考天津卷】

3D food printing *still* has challenges *to overcome*.

Currently, most ingredients must be changed to a paste *first*,

and the printing process is *quite* time-consuming. *Besides*,

most of the 3D food printers *now* are restricted *to dry*

ingredients **because** meat and milk products may easily go

bad. Some experts think 3D food printers are *better suited*

for fast food restaurants **than** homes and high-end restaurants.

　　3D 食品列印還有一些挑戰要克服。目前，大部分的原料必須先變成糊狀物，而且列印的過程相當費時。此外，大部分的 3D 食品列印機現在受限於乾燥的原料，因爲肉類和乳製品可能很容易腐壞。有些專家認爲，比起住家和高檔的餐廳，3D 食品列印機更適合速食餐廳。

* printing〔ˈprɪntɪŋ〕*n.* 列印　　challenge〔ˈtʃælɪndʒ〕*n.* 挑戰
　overcome〔ˌovɚˈkʌm〕*v.* 征服；克服
　currently〔ˈkɝəntlɪ〕*adv.* 目前；現在
　ingredient〔ɪnˈgridɪənt〕*n.* 成分；原料
　change〔tʃendʒ〕*v.* 改變　　paste〔pest〕*n.* 糊狀物
　process〔ˈprɑsɛs〕*n.* 過程　　quite〔kwaɪt〕*adv.* 十分；相當
　time-consuming〔ˈtaɪmkənˌsumɪŋ〕*adj.* 費時的

besides〔 bɪˋsaɪdz 〕 *adv.* 此外　　printer〔ˋprɪntɚ〕 *n.* 印表機

restrict〔 rɪˋstrɪkt 〕 *v.* 限制　　dry〔 draɪ 〕 *adj.* 乾燥的

meat〔 mit 〕 *n.* 肉　　product〔ˋprɑdəkt〕 *n.* 產物；產品

go bad 壞掉　　expert〔ˋɛkspɝt〕 *n.* 專家

suited〔ˋsutɪd〕 *adj.* 適合的　　***fast food*** 速食

high-end〔ˋhaɪˌɛnd〕 *adj.* 高端的；高檔的

1. (**B**) What is the main factor that prevents 3D food printing from spreading widely?

　　使 3D 食品列印無法廣泛傳出去的主要因素為何？

　　(A) 3D food printers are too expensive.

　　　　3D 食品列印機太貴了。

　　(B) The printing process is long and complicated.

　　　　<u>列印過程很漫長而且複雜。</u>

　　* main〔 men 〕 *adj.* 主要的　　factor〔ˋfæktɚ〕 *n.* 因素

　　　prevent〔 prɪˋvɛnt 〕 *v.* 阻止；妨礙 < *from* >

　　　spread〔 sprɛd 〕 *v.* 散播；傳播

　　　widely〔ˋwaɪdlɪ〕 *adv.* 廣泛地

　　　complicated〔ˋkɑmpləˌketɪd〕 *adj.* 複雜的

TEST 27 詳解

【 **2018 高考浙江卷** 】

Look at reusable shopping bags. ***The stronger a reusable bag is***, the longer its life **and** the more plastic-bag use *it* *cancels out. However,* longer-lasting reusable bags *often*

require more energy *to make.* A cotton bag must be used *at*

least 131 times to be better for the planet than plastic.

　　看看可重複使用的購物袋。可重複使用的袋子（環保購物袋）越堅固，使用壽命越長，就可以抵銷掉越多的塑膠袋使用。然而，比較持久的環保購物袋，製造時通常需要更多的能量。棉布袋至少必須使用 131 次，才會比塑膠袋對地球更好。

* reusable〔rɪˈjuzəbḷ〕*adj.* 可重複使用的
  shopping bag 購物袋
  the + 比較級…***the*** + 比較級… 越…就越…
  plastic〔ˈplæstɪk〕*n., adj.* 塑膠（的）
  cancel〔ˈkænsḷ〕*v.* 取消　　***cancel out*** 抵銷；平衡
  long-lasting〔ˈlɔŋˌlæstɪŋ〕*adj.* 持久的
  require〔rɪˈkwaɪr〕*v.* 需要　　energy〔ˈɛnədʒɪ〕*n.* 能量
  cotton〔ˈkɑtṇ〕*adj.* 棉（製）的　　***at least*** 至少
  planet〔ˈplænɪt〕*n.* 行星；此指「地球」

1. (**B**) What is a disadvantage of reusable bags?
　　環保購物袋的缺點是什麼？

　(A) They are less strong than plastic bags.
　　　它們沒有塑膠袋那樣堅固。

　(B) Producing them requires more energy.
　　　製造它們需要更多的能量。

* disadvantage〔ˌdɪsədˈvæntɪdʒ〕*n.* 缺點
  produce〔prəˈdjus〕*v.* 製造；生產

TEST 28

【2018 高考天津卷】

The pressures of "time" and "destination" are blocks to awareness. Many hikers head to a distant campground with just enough time to get there before dark. It seldom occurs to them to take a moment to see what's around them. When they are asked what they've seen, they say, "Oh, a few birds." They seem bent on reaching their destinations.

1. Why do the hikers take no notice of the surroundings during the journey?

   A. The natural beauty isn't attractive to them.

   B. They focus on arriving at the camp in time.

TEST 28 詳解

【2018 高考天津卷】

The pressures *of "time" and "destination"* are blocks to
S.   V.

awareness. Many hikers head to a distant campground *with*

just enough time to get there before dark. It *seldom* occurs to
虛主詞

them [*to take a moment to see **what**'s around them*.] ***When** they*
真　正　主　詞

*are asked **what** they've seen*, they say, "Oh, a few birds."

They seem bent on reaching their destinations.

「時間」和「目的地」的壓力會阻礙意識。許多健行者前往遙遠的露營地，時間剛好足夠在天黑以前到達。他們很少想到，要花一點時間看看周遭環境。當他們被問到他們看到了什麼，他們說：「噢，就一些鳥。」他們似乎只專注於到達他們的目的地。

* pressure〔'prɛʃɚ〕 *n.* 壓力
  destination〔,dɛstə'neʃən〕 *n.* 目的地
  block〔blɑk〕 *n.* 障礙物
  awareness〔ə'wɛrnɪs〕 *n.* 察覺；意識
  hiker〔'haɪkɚ〕 *n.* 健行者　　head〔hɛd〕 *v.* 前往
  distant〔'dɪstənt〕 *adj.* 遙遠的
  campground〔'kæmp,graʊnd〕 *n.* 露營地

dark〔dɑrk〕*n.* 黑暗；天黑　　***before dark*** 天黑以前
seldom〔'sɛldəm〕*adv.* 很少　　occur〔ə'kɝ〕*v.* 發生
*sth. **occur to** sb.* 某人想到某事
moment〔'momənt〕*n.* 時刻；時間
bent〔bɛnt〕*adj.* 專心⋯的；熱心⋯的 < *on* >
reach〔ritʃ〕*v.* 到達（= *get to* ）

1. (**B**) Why do the hikers take no notice of the surroundings
   during the journey?
   為什麼健行者在旅途中沒有注意周遭環境？

   (A) The natural beauty isn't attractive to them.
   　　自然的美景對他們沒有吸引力。

   (B) They focus on arriving at the camp in time.
   　　他們專注於及時抵達營地。

   * notice〔'notɪs〕*n.* 注意；留意
   take (no) notice of （不）注意
   surroundings〔sə'raundɪŋz〕*n. pl.* 周遭環境
   during〔'djurɪŋ〕*prep.* 在⋯期間
   journey〔'dʒɝnɪ〕*n.* 旅行；旅途
   natural〔'nætʃərəl〕*adj.* 自然的
   beauty〔'bjutɪ〕*n.* 美
   attractive〔ə'træktɪv〕*adj.* 吸引人的
   focus〔'fokəs〕*v.* 專注於 < *on* >
   arrive〔ə'raɪv〕*v.* 到達
   camp〔kæmp〕*n.* 營地　　***in time*** 及時

TEST 29

【2018 高考浙江卷】

Most experts date the first English novel to *Robinson Crusoe* in 1719. But 100 years later, there were still very few professional writers. The literacy rate in England was under 50%. Many works of fiction appeared without the names of the authors, often with something like "By a lady." Novels, for the most part, were looked upon as silly, immoral or just plain bad.

1. Which of the following best describes British novels in the 18th century?

   A. They were popular among the rich.

   B. They were seen as nearly worthless.

TEST 29 詳解

【2018 高考浙江卷】

Most experts date the first English novel *to Robinson Crusoe in 1719.* ***But*** *100 years later*, there were *still* very few professional writers. The literacy rate *in England* was under 50%. Many works of fiction appeared *without the names of the authors*, *often with something like "By a lady."* Novels, *for the most part*, were looked upon as silly, immoral or *just* plain bad.

　　大部分的專家斷定,第一部英文小說是 1719 年的「魯濱遜漂流記」。但是一百年之後,職業作家依然很少。英國的識字率不到百分之50。許多小說出版,都沒有寫出作者的名字,通常只標註「一位女士著」。當時小說多半是認為是愚蠢的,不道德的,或僅僅就是不好的。

* expert〔ˈɛkspɝt〕*n.* 專家　　date〔det〕*v.* 斷定年代
  novel〔ˈnɑvḷ〕*n.* 小說
  Robinson Crusoe〔ˈrɑbɪnsṇˈkruso〕*n.* 魯濱遜漂流記【首次出版於 1719 年,作者為丹尼爾‧笛福（Daniel Defoe〔ˈdænjəl dɪˈfo〕）,敘述海難倖存者魯濱遜,在一個偏僻荒涼的小島上度過 28 年的故事】
  professional〔prəˈfɛʃənḷ〕*adj.* 職業的
  writer〔ˈraɪtɚ〕*n.* 作家　　literacy〔ˈlɪtərəsɪ〕*n.* 讀寫的能力

rate〔ret〕*n.* 率；比例　　work〔wɜk〕*n.* 作品

fiction〔'fɪkʃən〕*n.* 小說　　appear〔ə'pɪr〕*v.* 出現

author〔'ɔθɚ〕*n.* 作者　　***for the most part*** 大部分；多半

look upon A as B 認為 A 是 B

be looked upon as 被認為是～　　silly〔'sɪlɪ〕*adj.* 愚蠢的

immoral〔ɪ'mɔrəl〕*adj.* 不道德的

just〔dʒʌst〕*adv.* 就是；僅僅

plain〔plen〕*adv.* 清楚地；完全地

1. (**B**) Which of the following best describes British novels
in the 18th century?

下列何者最能敘述十八世紀的英國小說？

(A) They were popular among the rich.

它們受到有錢人的歡迎。

(B) They were seen as nearly worthless.

<u>它們被認為是幾乎無價值的。</u>

* following〔'faloɪŋ〕*n.* 下列

describe〔dɪ'skraɪb〕*v.* 描寫；敘述

British〔'brɪtɪʃ〕*adj.* 英國的

century〔'sɛntʃərɪ〕*n.* 世紀

popular〔'pɑpjəlɚ〕*adj.* 受歡迎的

be popular among/with ～　受～歡迎

see A as B 認為 A 是 B (= *look upon A as B*)

be seen as 被視為～；被認為是～ (= *be looked upon as*)

nearly〔'nɪrlɪ〕*adv.* 將近；幾乎

worthless〔'wɜθlɪs〕*adj.* 無價值的

TEST 30

【2018 高考全國卷】

There is clear evidence of parents serving as examples and important guides for their kids when it comes to reading. Data shows that kids and teens who read frequently have more books at home, more books purchased for them, parents who read more often, and parents who set aside time for them to read.

1. How should parents encourage their children to read more?

   A. Act as role models for them.

   B. Ask them to write book reports.

TEST 31

【2018 高考浙江卷】

Modern America was born on the road, behind a wheel. The car shaped some of the most lasting aspects of American culture: the roadside diner, the billboard, the motel, even the hamburger. For most of the last century, the car represented what it meant to be American—going forward at high speed to find new worlds.

1. Why is the hamburger mentioned in the paragraph?
   A. To explain Americans' love for traveling by car.
   B. To show the influence of cars on American culture.

TEST 30 詳解

【2018 高考全國卷】

There is clear evidence *of parents serving as examples*
and important guides for their kids **when** it comes to reading.
Data shows **that** kids and teens **who** read frequently have
　　　　　　　　　　　主 詞
more books at home, more books purchased for them, parents
who read more often, **and** parents **who** set aside time for them
to read.

　　有明顯的證據證明，一提到閱讀，父母親要作孩子的模範和重要的
引導者。資料顯示，經常閱讀的小孩和青少年，家裡有比較多的書，比
較多為他們買的書，他們的父母也比較常閱讀，還有他們的父母會保留
給他們閱讀的時間。

* clear〔klɪr〕*adj.* 明顯的　　evidence〔'ɛvədəns〕*n.* 證據
  serve as 當作；充當　　example〔ɪg'zæmpḷ〕*n.* 例子；模範
  guide〔gaɪd〕*n.* 指導者；引導者　　kid〔kɪd〕*n.* 小孩
  when it comes to N/V-ing 一提到～　　data〔'detə〕*n.* 資料
  teens〔tinz〕*n., pl.* 十幾歲的青少年
  frequently〔'frikwəntlɪ〕*adv.* 經常地
  purchase〔'pɝtʃəs〕*v.* 購買（= *buy*）　　***set aside*** 保留；挪開

1. (**A**) How should parents encourage their children to read more?　父母親如何鼓勵他們的孩子多閱讀？

    (A) Act as role models for them.　當他們的榜樣。

    (B) Ask them to write book reports.

        要求他們寫讀書報告。

    * encourage〔 ɪnˋkɝɪdʒ 〕*v.* 鼓勵；勉勵

      act as 充當；擔任　　role〔 rol 〕*n.* 角色

      model〔ˋmɑdḷ〕*n.* 模型；模範　　***role model*** 模範

      report〔 rɪˋport 〕*n.* 報告

TEST 31 詳解

【2018 高考浙江卷】

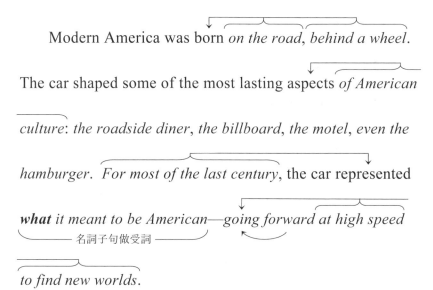

Modern America was born *on the road, behind a wheel.*

The car shaped some of the most lasting aspects *of American*

culture: *the roadside diner, the billboard, the motel, even the*

hamburger. For most of the last century, the car represented

what *it meant to be American*—*going forward at high speed*

    —— 名詞子句做受詞 ——

to find new worlds.

現代美國是在道路上，在方向盤後面誕生的。美國文化中最持久的幾個方面，是汽車塑造出來的：路邊的餐館、路邊大型的廣告看板、汽車旅館，甚至是漢堡。在上個世紀大部分的時間裡，汽車都代表了美國的意義——高速前進以尋找新世界。

* modern〔ˋmɑdɚn〕*adj.* 現代的
  behind〔bɪˋhaɪnd〕*prep.* 在…之後
  wheel〔hwil〕*n.* 輪子；方向盤
  behind the wheel 坐在方向盤後面；開車中
  shape〔ʃep〕*v.* 塑造　　lasting〔ˋlæstɪŋ〕*adj.* 持久的
  aspect〔ˋæspɛkt〕*n.* 方面　　culture〔ˋkʌltʃɚ〕*n.* 文化
  roadside〔ˋrod͵saɪd〕*adj.* 路邊的；路旁的
  diner〔ˋdaɪnɚ〕*n.* 用餐者；餐車；餐車式餐館
  billboard〔ˋbɪl͵bord〕*n.* 廣告看板；告示板
  motel〔moˋtɛl〕*n.* 汽車旅館
  hamburger〔ˋhæmbɝgɚ〕*n.* 漢堡
  century〔ˋsɛntʃərɪ〕*n.* 世紀　　represent〔͵rɛprɪˋzɛnt〕*v.* 代表
  mean〔min〕*v.* 意義；意味　　forward〔ˋfɔrwɚd〕*adv.* 向前地
  speed〔spid〕*n.* 速度　　***at high speed*** 以高速

1.(**B**) Why is the hamburger mentioned in the paragraph?
　　　　這個段落為什麼會提到漢堡？

　　(A) To explain Americans' love for traveling by car.
　　　　為了解釋美國人對開車旅行的愛好。

　　(B) To show the influence of cars on American culture.
　　　　<u>為了顯示汽車對美國文化的影響。</u>

　　* mention〔ˋmɛnʃən〕*v.* 提到
　　　paragraph〔ˋpærə͵græf〕*n.* 段落
　　　explain〔ɪkˋsplen〕*v.* 解釋；說明
　　　travel〔ˋtrævl̩〕*v.* 旅行　　influence〔ˋɪnfluəns〕*n.* 影響

TEST 32

【2018 高考浙江卷】

Charles Dickens led an explosion in the publication of novels and was hailed as the first professional writer. Today Dickens' greatness is unchallenged. Removing him from the English literature hall of fame would make about as much sense as the Louvre selling off the *Mona Lisa*.

1. Dickens is compared with the Mona Lisa to stress _____.

   A. his success in publication

   B. his importance in literature

TEST 33

【2018 高考江蘇卷】

Time is money, but that principle means different things for different types of restaurants. One way for fine dining restaurants to encourage customers to stay longer and order more: put on some Mozart. When classical music, rather than pop music, was playing, diners spent more. Fast music hurried diners out.

1. How could a fine dining restaurant make more money?

   A. Play classical music.

   B. Introduce pop music.

TEST 32 詳解

【2018 高考浙江卷】

Charles Dickens led an explosion *in the publication of*

novels **and** was hailed as the first professional writer. *Today*

Dickens' greatness is unchallenged. Removing him *from the*
主　詞

English literature hall of fame would make *about as much*

sense **as** *the Louvre selling off the Mona Lisa.*

　　查爾斯·狄更斯帶領了小說出版的大爆炸，被譽為是第一位職業作家。今日，狄更斯的偉大無人能挑戰。把他從英國文學名人堂除名，意義和羅浮宮把蒙娜麗莎廉售出去差不多。

* Charles Dickens〔'tʃɑrlz'dɪkɪnz〕*n.* 查爾斯·狄更斯【1812-1870，
　　是 19 世紀維多利亞時代的文學家，是英國最偉大的作家之一】
lead〔lid〕*v.* 領導　　explosion〔ɪk'sploʒən〕*n.* 爆發
publication〔͵pʌblɪ'keʃən〕*n.* 出版；發行
novel〔'nɑvl̩〕*n.* 小說　　hail〔hel〕*v.* 歡呼；致敬
be hailed as 被譽為　　professional〔prə'fɛʃənl̩〕*adj.* 職業的
writer〔'raɪtɚ〕*n.* 作家　　greatness〔'gretnɪs〕*n.* 偉大；卓越
unchallenged〔ʌn'tʃælɪndʒd〕*adj.* 未受到挑戰的；未引起爭論的
remove〔rɪ'muv〕*v.* 除去　　literature〔'lɪtərətʃɚ〕*n.* 文學
hall〔hɔl〕*n.* 大廳　　fame〔fem〕*n.* 名聲；聲譽

hall of fame 榮譽廳；名人堂　　***make sense*** 合理；有意義

the Louvre〔ˈluvɚ〕*n.* 羅浮宮

【位於巴黎，是全世界最大的藝術

　博物館，也是參觀人次最多的，

　主要收藏 1860 年前的藝術作品與

　考古文物】　　***sell off*** 廉售（庫存、所有物等）

the Mona Lisa〔ˈmonəˈlizə〕*n.* 蒙娜麗莎

【義大利藝術家達文西（Leonardo da

　Vinci〔ˌliɑˈnɑrdodəˈvɪntʃɪ〕）所畫的

　肖像畫，是全世界最著名的油畫之一，

　收藏於巴黎羅浮宮】

1.（ **B** ）Dickens is compared with the Mona Lisa to stress ＿＿＿＿.
　　狄更斯被拿來和蒙娜麗莎比較，是為了強調 ＿＿＿＿＿＿。

　　(A) his success in publication. 他在出版界的成功

　　(B) his importance in literature. 他在文學界的重要性

　　* compare〔kəmˈpɛr〕*v.* 比較 <*with* >
　　　stress〔strɛs〕*v.* 強調　　success〔səkˈsɛs〕*n.* 成功
　　　importance〔ɪmˈpɔrtn̩s〕*n.* 重要性

TEST 33 詳解

【2018 高考江蘇卷】

Time is money, ***but*** that principle means different things

for different types of restaurants. One way *for fine dining* *restaurants to encourage customers to stay longer **and** order*

more: put on some Mozart. ***When** classical music, rather than*

pop music, was playing, diners spent more. Fast music hurried

diners *out*.

　　時間就是金錢，但這個原則在不同類型的餐廳裡，可能意味著不同的事情。好的餐廳鼓勵客人待久一點、點多一點的方法之一，就是播放莫札特的音樂。當餐廳播放古典音樂，而不是流行音樂時，用餐者會多消費一點。節奏快的音樂會催促用餐者離開。

* ***Time is money.*** 時間就是金錢。
principle〔ˈprɪnsəbḷ〕*n.* 原則　　type〔taɪp〕*n.* 種類
encourage〔ɪnˈkɝɪdʒ〕*v.* 鼓勵
customer〔ˈkʌstəmɚ〕*n.* 顧客　　order〔ˈɔrdɚ〕*v.* 點餐
put on 播放 (= *play*)
Mozart〔ˈmozɑrt〕*n.* 莫札特【1756-1791，奧地利作曲家】；
　　此指莫札特的音樂　　classical〔ˈklæsɪkḷ〕*adj.* 古典的
rather than 而不是　　***pop music*** 流行音樂
diner〔ˈdaɪnɚ〕*n.* 用餐者　　hurry〔ˈhɝɪ〕*v.* 催促

1. (**A**) How could a fine dining restaurant make more money?
　　一家好的餐廳如何能夠賺更多錢？
　　(A) Play classical music. 播放古典音樂。
　　(B) Introduce pop music. 介紹流行音樂。
　　* ***make money*** 賺錢　　introduce〔ˌɪntrəˈdjus〕*v.* 介紹

TEST 34

【2018 高考全國卷】

When the world was still populated by hunter-gatherers, small tightly-knit groups developed their own patterns of speech. Some language experts believe that 10,000 years ago, when the world had just five to ten million people, they spoke perhaps 12,000 languages between them.

1. What can we infer about languages in hunter-gatherer times?

   A. They developed very fast.

   B. They were large in number.

TEST 34 詳解

【2018 高考全國卷】

> ***When*** the world was still populated by hunter-gatherers,
>
> small tightly-knit groups developed their own patterns *of*
>
> *speech.* Some language experts believe ***that*** 10,000 years ago,
>
> *when* the world had just five to ten million people, they spoke
>
> *perhaps 12,000 languages between them.*

　　當這個世界住的仍然是採獵者時，緊密結合的小團體，會發展出他們自己的語言模式。有些語言專家相信，在一萬年前，當全世界只有五百到一千萬人口時，人與人之間所說的語言也許有一萬二千種。

* populate〔'pɑpjə‚let〕v. 居住於
hunter-gatherer〔'hʌntɚ‚gæðərɚ〕n. 採獵者
tightly〔'taɪtlɪ〕adv. 緊緊地　　knit〔nɪt〕v. 編織；結合
tightly-knit adj. 緊密結合的　　develop〔dɪ'vɛləp〕v. 發展
pattern〔'pætɚn〕n. 模式；型態　　speech〔spitʃ〕n. 言語
expert〔'ɛkspɝt〕n. 專家　　perhaps〔pɚ'hæps〕adv. 也許

1. (**B**) What can we infer about languages in hunter-gatherer
times? 在採獵者時期，關於語言我們可以推論出什麼？
(A) They developed very fast. 它們發展非常快速。
(B) They were large in number. 它們數目眾多。

* infer〔ɪn'fɝ〕v. 推論

TEST 35

【2018 高考全國卷】

Most people think we get rid of our worn technology at the first sight of something new, but a new study shows that we keep using our old devices well after they go out of style. That's bad news for the environment as these outdated devices consume much more energy than the newer ones.

1. What does the author think of new devices?

   A. They are environment-friendly.

   B. They cost more to use at home.

TEST 36

【2018 高考全國卷】

When combined with berries or slices of other fruits, frozen bananas make an excellent base for thick fruit shakes. Remove the skin of ripe bananas and place them in containers and freeze. A squeeze of fresh lemon juice on the bananas will prevent them from turning brown. Frozen bananas will last weeks, depending on their ripeness and the temperature of the freezer.

1. Why is fresh lemon juice used in freezing bananas?

  A. To keep their color.

  B. To speed up their ripening.

TEST 35 詳解

【2018 高考全國卷】

Most people think we get rid of our worn technology *at the first sight of something new*, **but** a new study shows **that** we keep using our old devices well **after** they go out of style.

That's bad news *for the environment* **as** these outdated devices consume much more energy than the newer ones.

　　大部分人認為，我們第一眼看到新的東西，就會把我們用舊了的科技產品丟掉，但一項新的研究顯示，我們會一直使用舊裝置，直到它們不再流行為止。那對環境而言是個壞消息，因為這些過時的裝置比新裝置，消耗更多的能源。

> * ***get rid of*** 除去；丟掉　　worn〔worn〕*adj.* 用舊了的
> technology〔tɛk'nɑlədʒɪ〕*n.* 科技
> ***at the first sight of*** 第一眼看到
> study〔'stʌdɪ〕*n.* 研究　　device〔dɪ'vaɪs〕*n.* 裝置
> style〔staɪl〕*n.* 流行款式　　***out of style*** 不流行
> environment〔ɪn'vaɪrənmənt〕*n.* 環境
> outdated〔aʊt'detɪd〕*adj.* 過時的；落伍的
> consume〔kən'sum〕*v.* 消耗　　energy〔'ɛnədʒɪ〕*n.* 能源

1. (**A**) What does the author think of new devices?

作者對新的裝置有何看法？

(A) They are environment-friendly. <u>它們符合環保。</u>

(B) They cost more to use at home.

它們在家使用花費更多。

* author〔'ɔθɚ〕*n.* 作者   ***think of*** 認為

environment-friendly〔ɪn'vaɪrənmənt'frɛndlɪ〕

adj. 對環境友善的；符合環保的

TEST 36 詳解

【 2018 高考全國卷 】

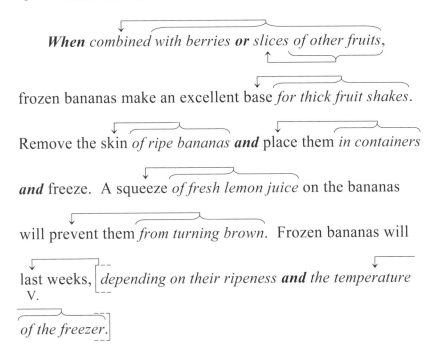

When combined with berries or slices of other fruits,

frozen bananas make an excellent base for thick fruit shakes.

Remove the skin of ripe bananas and place them in containers

and freeze. A squeeze of fresh lemon juice on the bananas

will prevent them from turning brown. Frozen bananas will

last weeks, depending on their ripeness and the temperature
V.

of the freezer.

　　和漿果或其他水果切片組合在一起時，冷凍香蕉是絕佳的基底，可以做成濃郁的水果奶昔。成熟的香蕉把皮剝掉，放在容器裡加以冷凍。香蕉上擠一些新鮮的檸檬汁，可以防止香蕉變黑。冷凍的香蕉可以存放數週之久，取決於香蕉的成熟度和冷凍庫的溫度。

* combine〔kəm'baɪn〕v. 結合；組合
berry〔'bɛrɪ〕n. 莓果；漿果　　slice〔slaɪs〕n. 薄片；切片
frozen〔'frozn̩〕adj. 冷凍的
excellent〔'ɛksḷənt〕adj. 絕佳的；極好的
base〔bes〕n. 基礎；基底　　thick〔θɪk〕adj. 濃的
shake〔ʃek〕n. 奶昔　　remove〔rɪ'muv〕v. 除去
skin〔skɪn〕n.（蔬果等的）薄皮
ripe〔raɪp〕adj. 成熟的　　place〔ples〕v. 放置
container〔kən'tenɚ〕n. 容器
freeze〔friz〕v. 結冰；冰凍
squeeze〔skwiz〕n. 壓榨；（少量的）榨汁
fresh〔frɛʃ〕adj. 新鮮的　　lemon〔'lɛmən〕n. 檸檬
juice〔dʒus〕n. 果汁
prevent〔prɪ'vɛnt〕v. 阻止；防止 <from>
last〔læst〕v. 持續　　*depend on* 視～而定；取決於
ripeness〔'raɪpnɪs〕n. 成熟
temperature〔'tɛmpərətʃɚ〕n. 溫度
freezer〔'frizɚ〕n. 冷凍庫

1. (**A**) Why is fresh lemon juice used in freezing bananas?
爲什麼冷凍香蕉時要使用新鮮的檸檬汁？

(A) To keep their color. <u>爲了保留它們的顏色。</u>

(B) To speed up their ripening. 爲了加速它們的成熟。

* *speed up* 加速　　ripen〔'raɪpən〕v. 成熟；變熟

TEST 37

【2018 高考江蘇卷】

Things you might expect to discourage spending—"bad" tables and crowding—don't necessarily. Diners at bad tables—next to the kitchen door, say—spent nearly as much as others but soon fled. As for crowds, they were found to increase a restaurant's reputation, suggesting great food at fair prices.

1. What does the paragraph talk about?

   A. Problems restaurants are faced with.

   B. Common misunderstandings about restaurants.

TEST 38

【2017 高考全國卷】

I work with Volunteers for Wildlife, a rescue and education organization. Trying to help injured or sick creatures can be heartbreaking; survival is never certain. However, when it works, it is simply beautiful.

1. What is unavoidable in the author's rescue work according the paragraph?

   A. Efforts made in vain.

   B. Getting injured in his work.

TEST 37 詳解

【2018 高考江蘇卷】

Things *you might expect to discourage spending*—"bad"
S.

tables and crowding—don't necessarily. Diners *at bad*
V.

tables—next to the kitchen door, say—spent *nearly* as much

as others ***but*** *soon* fled. *As for crowds,* they were found to

increase a restaurant's reputation, *suggesting great food at*

fair prices.

　　有些情況，你預期可能會使顧客打消念頭不來消費的——「不好」
的位子和擁擠——不一定會。座位不好的用餐者——比如坐在廚房門旁
邊——消費和其他人一樣多，但是很快就會離開了。至於人群，被發現
可以增加餐廳的名聲，顯示這裡的平價美食。

　　* expect〔ɪkˋspɛkt〕v. 期待；預期
　　　discourage〔dɪsˋkɝɪdʒ〕v. 使氣餒；使打消念頭
　　　crowding〔ˋkraʊdɪŋ〕n. 擁擠
　　　necessarily〔ˋnɛsə͵sɛrəlɪ〕adv. 必定；必然
　　　not necessarily 不一定；未必
　　　diner〔ˋdaɪnɚ〕n. 用餐者　　***next to*** 在～隔壁
　　　say〔se〕v. 說；例如；大約【常插入句中，用於數字或例子】
　　　nearly〔ˋnɪrlɪ〕adv. 接近；差不多　　flee〔fli〕v. 逃離；離開

as for 至於　　crowd〔kraʊd〕*n.* 群眾；人群　*v.* 群集；擠滿
reputation〔ˏrɛpjəˈteʃən〕*n.* 名聲；名譽
suggest〔sə(g)ˈdʒɛst〕*v.* 顯示；暗示
fair〔fɛr〕*adj.* 合理的；公道的

1.(**B**) What does the paragraph talk about?　這個段落談論什麼？
　(A) Problems restaurants are faced with.
　　　餐廳面臨的問題。
　(B) Common misunderstandings about restaurants.
　　　對餐廳常見的誤解。

　＊paragraph〔ˈpærəˏgræf〕*n.* 段落
　　talk about 談論；討論　　*be faced with* 面臨
　　common〔ˈkɑmən〕*adj.* 一般的；常見的
　　misunderstanding〔ˏmɪsʌndəˈstændɪŋ〕*n.* 誤解；誤會

TEST 38 詳解

【2017 高考全國卷】

I work *with Volunteers for Wildlife*, *a rescue **and** education*
　　　　　　　　　　　　　　　　　　　　　同 位 語

organization. Trying to help injured or sick creatures can
　　　　　　　　　　　主　詞

be heartbreaking; survival is *never* certain. *However*, **when** *it*

works, it is *simply* beautiful.

　　我在「野生動物志願者公司」工作，這是一個救援和教育組織。試著幫助受傷或生病的動物，可能會令人心碎；生還從來不確定。然而，救援順利時，那就太美了。

　　* volunteer〔,vɑlən'tɪr〕*n.* 志願者；自願者
　　wildlife〔'waɪld,laɪf〕*n.* 野生生物　　rescue〔'rɛskju〕*n.* 救援
　　education〔,ɛdʒə'keʃən〕*n.* 教育
　　organization〔,ɔrgənə'zeʃən〕*n.* 組織
　　injured〔'ɪndʒəd〕*adj.* 受傷的　　creature〔'kritʃə〕*n.* 生物
　　heartbreaking〔'hɑrt,brekɪŋ〕*adj.* 令人心碎的【形容非人，
　　　形容人用 heartbroken】
　　survival〔sə'vaɪvḷ〕*n.* 生存；生還
　　certain〔'sɝtṇ〕*adj.* 確定的　　work〔wɝk〕*v.* 有效；順利
　　simply〔'sɪmplɪ〕*adv.* 的確；確實

1. (**A**) What is unavoidable in the author's rescue work
　　　　according the paragraph?
　　　　根據本段，在作者的救援工作中什麼是難以避免的？
　　　　(A) Efforts made in vain. 所做的努力徒勞無功。
　　　　(B) Getting injured in his work. 在工作中受傷。

　　　　* unavoidable〔,ʌnə'vɔɪdəbḷ〕*adj.* 難以避免的；無可逃避的
　　　　author〔'ɔθə〕*n.* 作者　　effort〔'ɛfət〕*n.* 努力
　　　　make efforts 努力　　vain〔ven〕*adj.* 徒勞的
　　　　in vain 徒勞無功地

TEST 39

【2017 高考全國卷】

Pacific Science Center has been inspiring a passion for discovery and lifelong learning in science, math and technology. Today, we serve more than 1.3 million people a year. It's an amazing accomplishment, and we could not have achieved it without generous support from individuals, corporations, and other social organizations. Visit our website to find various ways you can support us.

1. What is the purpose of the passage?

   A. To encourage donations.

   B. To tell about the Center's history.

TEST 39 詳解

【2017 高考全國卷】

Pacific Science Center has been inspiring a passion *for*

*discovery **and*** lifelong learning *in science, math **and***

technology. *Today*, we serve more than 1.3 million people

a year. It's an amazing accomplishment, ***and*** we could not

have achieved it *without generous support from individuals,*

*corporations, **and** other social organizations*. Visit our

website to find various ways *you can support us*.

　　「太平洋科學中心」一直以來，激勵了大家對發現的愛好，以及科學、數學及科技方面的終身學習。今日，我們每年服務超過一百三十萬人，這是個驚人的成就，而如果沒有個人、公司和其他社會團體的慷慨支持，我們是不可能達成的。請上我們的網站，找出您可以支持我們的各種方式。

　　* Pacific〔pəˋsɪfɪk〕*adj.* 太平洋的
　　　science〔ˋsaɪəns〕*n.* 科學　　center〔ˋsɛntɚ〕*n.* 中心
　　　inspire〔ɪnˋspaɪr〕*v.* 激發；鼓舞
　　　passion〔ˋpæʃən〕*n.* 激情；熱情
　　　discovery〔dɪˋskʌvrɪ〕*n.* 發現

lifelong〔'laɪf,lɔŋ〕*adj.* 一生的；終生的

math〔mæθ〕*n.* 數學

technology〔tɛk'nɑlədʒɪ〕*n.* 科技　　serve〔sɝv〕*v.* 服務

amazing〔ə'mezɪŋ〕*adj.* 驚人的；令人吃驚的

accomplishment〔ə'kɑmplɪʃmənt〕*n.* 成就；成果

achieve〔ə'tʃiv〕*v.* 完成；達到

generous〔'dʒɛnərəs〕*adj.* 大方的；慷慨的

support〔sə'port〕*n., v.* 支持；支撐

individual〔,ɪndə'vɪdʒʊəl〕*n.* 個人

corporation〔,kɔrpə'reʃən〕*n.* 財團法人

social〔'soʃəl〕*adj.* 社會的

organization〔,ɔrgənə'zeʃən〕*n.* 組織

website〔'wɛb,saɪt〕*n.* 網站

various〔'vɛrɪəs〕*adj.* 各種的

1. (**A**) What is the purpose of the passage?

　　這篇文章的目的是什麼？

　(A) To encourage donations.

　　　<u>鼓勵捐款。</u>

　(B) To tell about the Center's history.

　　　敘述關於中心的歷史。

　* purpose〔'pɝpəs〕*n.* 目的

　　passage〔'pæsɪdʒ〕*n.* 文章

　　encourage〔ɪn'kɝɪdʒ〕*v.* 鼓勵

　　donation〔do'neʃən〕*n.* 捐贈；捐款

　　history〔'hɪstrɪ〕*n.* 歷史

TEST 40

【2017 高考全國卷】

Some of the world's most famous musicians recently gathered to celebrate the first annual International Jazz Day. UNESCO (United Nations Educational, Scientific and Cultural Organization) recently set April 30 as a day to raise awareness of jazz music, its significance, and its potential as a unifying voice across cultures.

1. Why did UNESCO set April 30 as International Jazz Day?
   A. To encourage people to study music.
   B. To recognize the value of jazz.

TEST 40 詳解

【2017 高考全國卷】

Some of the world's most famous musicians *recently*

gathered *to celebrate the first annual International Jazz Day.*

UNESCO (*United Nations Educational, Scientific and*

Cultural Organization) *recently* set April 30 as a day *to raise*

awareness *of jazz music, its significance,* **and** *its potential as*

a unifying voice across cultures.

　　一些全世界最知名的音樂家最近齊聚一堂，來慶祝第一屆年度「國際爵士樂日」。聯合國教育、科學及文化組織，最近決定四月 30 日這一天為國際爵士樂日，以提高大家對於爵士樂、它的重要性，以及它有潛力作為跨越文化一個統一的聲音的意識。

* famous〔ˈfeməs〕*adj.* 有名的
　recently〔ˈrisn̩tlɪ〕*adv.* 最近；近來
　gather〔ˈgæðɚ〕*v.* 集合；聚集
　celebrate〔ˈsɛləˌbret〕*v.* 慶祝
　annual〔ˈænjʊəl〕*adj.* 每年的；年度的
　international〔ˌɪntɚˈnæʃən̩l〕*adj.* 國際的
　jazz〔dʒæz〕*n.* 爵士樂
　UNESCO〔juˈnɛsko〕*n.* 聯合國教科文組織

united〔ju'naɪtɪd〕*adj.* 聯合的

nation〔'neʃən〕*n.* 國家　　***United Nations*** 聯合國

educational〔͵ɛdʒə'keʃənḷ〕*adj.* 教育的

scientific〔͵saɪən'tɪfɪk〕*adj.* 科學的

cultural〔'kʌltʃərəl〕*adj.* 文化的

organization〔͵ɔrgənə'zeʃən〕*n.* 組織

set〔sɛt〕*v.* 決定；指定　　raise〔rez〕*v.* 提高

awareness〔ə'wɛrnɪs〕*n.* 意識

significance〔sɪg'nɪfəkəns〕*n.* 重要；重要性

potential〔pə'tɛnʃəl〕*n.* 可能性；潛力

unifying〔'junə͵faɪɪŋ〕*adj.* 統一的

across〔ə'krɔs〕*prep.* 跨越

culture〔'kʌltʃɚ〕*n.* 文化

1. (**B**) Why did UNESCO set April 30 as International Jazz
Day?

為什麼聯合國教科文組織要決定 4 月 30 日為國際爵士日？

(A) To encourage people to study music.

鼓勵人們去研讀音樂。

(B) To recognize the value of jazz.

<u>認可爵士樂的價值。</u>

* encourage〔ɪn'kɝɪdʒ〕*v.* 鼓勵；勉勵

recognize〔'rɛkəg͵naɪz〕*v.* 承認；認可

value〔'vælju〕*n.* 價值

TEST 41

【2017 高考全國卷】

A build-it-yourself solar still is one of the best ways to obtain drinking water in areas where the liquid is not readily available. Developed in the U.S., it's an excellent water collector. You must carry the necessary equipment with you, since it's all but impossible to find natural substitutes. Fortunately the pieces required can be folded into a neat little pack and fastened on your belt.

1. What do we know about the solar still equipment from the paragraph?

    A. It's readily available.

    B. It's portable.

TEST 41 詳解

【2017 高考全國卷】

A build-it-yourself solar still is one of the best ways *to obtain drinking water in areas **where** the liquid is not readily available.* *Developed in the U.S.*, it's an excellent water collector. You must carry the necessary equipment *with you*, **since** *it's all but impossible to find natural substitutes.* *Fortunately* the pieces *required* can be folded *into a neat little pack* **and** fastened *on your belt.*

　　在飲用水不容易取得的地方，自製的太陽能蒸餾器，是取得飲用水最好的方法之一。這個裝置在美國被研發出來，是一個絕佳的集水器。你必須隨身帶著這個必要的裝備，因為幾乎不可能找到天然的替代品。幸好，這些必要的配件，可以被折入一個小小整齊的袋子裡，繫在皮帶上即可。

　　* solar〔'solɚ〕*adj.* 太陽（能）的
　　still〔stɪl〕*n.* 蒸餾器　　obtain〔əb'ten〕*v.* 獲得
　　drinking water 飲用水
　　area〔'ɛrɪə〕*n.* 地區；區域
　　liquid〔'lɪkwɪd〕*n.* 液體

readily〔'rɛdɪlɪ〕*adv.* 容易地；輕易地

available〔ə'veləbḷ〕*adj.* 可獲得的；有用的

develop〔dɪ'vɛləp〕*v.* 發展

excellent〔'ɛkslənt〕*adj.* 極佳的；極好的

collector〔kə'lɛktɚ〕*n.* 收集者；蒐集者

necessary〔'nɛsə,sɛrɪ〕*adj.* 必要的；必需的

equipment〔ɪ'kwɪpmənt〕*n.* 設備；器材

all but 幾乎（ = *nearly* = *almost* ）

natural〔'nætʃərəl〕*adj.* 自然的

substitute〔'sʌbstə,tut〕*n.* 替代品

fortunately〔'fɔrtʃənɪtlɪ〕*adv.* 幸運地

piece〔pis〕*n.* 破片；斷片

require〔rɪ'kwaɪr〕*v.* 要求；需要

fold〔fold〕*v.* 折疊

neat〔nit〕*adj.* 乾淨的；整齊的

pack〔pæk〕*n.* 包裹；一包

fasten〔'fæsṇ〕*v.* 綁緊；綁住

1. (**B**) What do we know about the solar still equipment from the paragraph?

從這個段落，關於這個太陽能蒸餾器，我們知道什麼？

(A) It's readily available. 它是容易取得的。

(B) It's portable. <u>它是可攜帶的。</u>

* paragraph〔'pærə,græf〕*n.* 段落
  portable〔'portəbḷ〕*adj.* 可攜帶的

TEST 42

【2017 高考全國卷】

Terrafugia Inc. said that its new flying car has completed its first flight. The vehicle—named the Transition— has two seats, four wheels and wings that fold up so it can be driven like a car. The Transition can reach around 70 miles per hour on the road and 115 in the air.

1. What is the paragraph mainly about?

A. The basic data of the Transition.

B. The advantages of flying cars.

TEST 43

【2017 高考全國卷】

Minutes after the last movie ended yesterday at the Plaza Theater, employees were busy cleaning up. The scene had been repeated many times in the theater's 75-year history. This time, however, was a little different. As one group of workers carried out the rubbish, another group began removing seats and other theater equipment in preparation for the building's end.

1. In what way was yesterday's cleanup at the Plaza special?

   A. It signaled the closedown of the theater.

   B. It marked the 75th anniversary of the theater.

TEST 42 詳解

【2017 高考全國卷】

Terrafugia Inc. said *that its new flying car has completed its first flight*. The vehicle—*named the Transition*—has two seats, four wheels *and* wings *that fold up so it can be driven like a car*. The Transition can reach around 70 miles *per hour on the road and* 115 *in the air*.

特拉弗吉亞有限公司宣稱，他們新研發的飛行汽車，已經完成第一次飛行測試。這輛車被命名為 Transition，有兩個座位、四個輪子，和可以收折起來的兩翼，所以可以像汽車一樣駕駛。Transition 飛行汽車在道路上行駛可以達到每小時 70 英哩，在空中飛行每小時 115 英哩。

* Terrafugia Inc. 〔ˏtɛrəˈfjudʒɪə〕*n.* 特拉弗吉亞有限公司【Inc. 為 Incorporated 的縮寫，要唸成〔ɪnˈkɔrpəˏretɪd〕，位於美國，研發飛行汽車的公司，2017 年被中國浙江吉利控股集團收購，成為其子公司】

flying car 飛行汽車　　complete〔kəmˈplit〕*v.* 完成

flight〔flaɪt〕*n.* 飛行　　vehicle〔ˈviɪk!〕*n.* 車輛

transition〔trænˈzɪʃən〕*n.* 過渡期；轉變

seat〔sit〕*n.* 座位；座椅

wheel〔hwil〕*n.* 車輪；輪子

wing〔wɪŋ〕*n.* 翼

fold〔fold〕*v.* 折疊 <*up*>

reach〔ritʃ〕*v.* 達到

1. (**A**) What is the paragraph mainly about?

這個段落主要在談論什麼？

(A) The basic data of the Transition.

<u>飛行汽車 Transition 的基本資料。</u>

(B) The advantages of flying cars. 飛行汽車的好處。

* paragraph〔'pærə,græf〕*n.* 段落

mainly〔'menlɪ〕*adv.* 主要地　　basic〔'besɪk〕*adj.* 基本的

data〔'detə〕*n.* 資料　　advantage〔əd'væntɪdʒ〕*n.* 優點

TEST 43 詳解

【2017 高考全國卷】

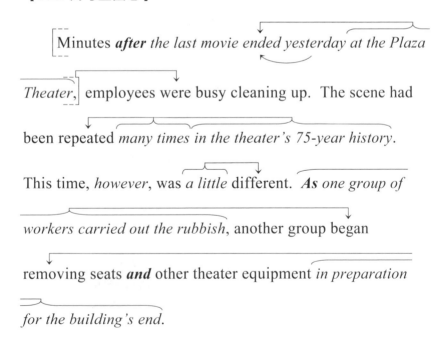

Minutes ***after*** *the last movie ended yesterday at the Plaza*

Theater, employees were busy cleaning up.　The scene had

been repeated *many times in the theater's 75-year history.*

This time, *however*, was *a little* different.　***As one group of***

workers carried out the rubbish, another group began

removing seats ***and*** other theater equipment *in preparation*

for the building's end.

　　昨天在廣場電影院，在最後一場電影結束後的幾分鐘，員工們忙著打掃。這個場景在電影院 75 年的歷史以來，已經重複很多遍了，然而，這一次有一點不一樣。當一群員工把垃圾清運出去時，另一群人開始拆除座椅和其他電影院的裝備，為這棟建築物的結束做準備。

　*　minute〔ˋmɪnɪt〕*n.* 分鐘　　end〔ɛnd〕*v., n.* 結束
　　plaza〔ˋplæzə , ˋplɑzə〕*n.* 廣場
　　theater〔ˋθiətɚ〕*n.* 劇院；電影院
　　employee〔͵ɛmplɔɪˋi〕*n.* 員工　　***be busy V-ing*** 忙於做某事
　　clean up 清掃；整理　　scene〔sin〕*n.* 場景
　　repeat〔rɪˋpit〕*v.* 重複　　history〔ˋhɪstrɪ〕*n.* 歷史
　　rubbish〔ˋrʌbɪʃ〕*n.* 垃圾；廢物
　　remove〔rɪˋmuv〕*v.* 移除；拆除　　seat〔sit〕*n.* 座位；座椅
　　equipment〔ɪˋkwɪpmənt〕*n.* 設備；器材
　　preparation〔͵prɛpəˋreʃən〕*n.* 準備；預備

1. (**A**)　In what way was yesterday's cleanup at the Plaza special?
　　廣場電影院昨天的大掃除在哪方面是特別的？
　　(A) It signaled the closedown of the theater.
　　　　這表示電影院要停業了。
　　(B) It marked the 75th anniversary of the theater.
　　　　這是要紀念電影院 75 週年紀念。

　*　cleanup〔ˋklin͵ʌp〕*n.* 大掃除
　　signal〔ˋsɪgnl̩〕*v.* 發信號；表示
　　closedown〔ˋkloz͵daʊn〕*n.* 停業；休業
　　mark〔mɑrk〕*v.* 作記號；紀念
　　anniversary〔͵ænəˋvɝsərɪ〕*n.* 週年紀念

TEST 44

【 2017 高考全國卷 】

A research team built a mobile laboratory named "DriveLAB" in order to understand the challenges older drivers face and to discover where the key stress points are. Research shows that giving up driving is one of the key reasons for a decline in health and well-being among older people, leading to them becoming more isolated and inactive.

1. What is the purpose of the DriveLAB?
   A. To find out older drivers' problems.
   B. To teach old people traffic rules.

TEST 45

【2017 高考北京卷】

On a cold March day, a softball team was practicing. Some girls were waiting for their next turns at bat, stamping their feet to stay warm. Suddenly, one of the girls, Paris White, fell to the ground. Her eyes rolled back. She started shaking. It was an emergency. She had suffered a sudden heart failure. Without immediate medical care, she would die.

1. What happened to Paris on a March day?

    A. She caught a bad cold.

    B. She had a sudden heart problem.

TEST 44 詳解

【2017 高考全國卷】

A research team built a mobile laboratory *named*

"*DriveLAB*" in order to understand the challenges *older*

drivers face *and* to discover [*where the key stress points are.*]
受詞

Research shows *that* [*giving up driving*] is one of the key
主詞

reasons for a decline in health and well-being among older

people, leading to them becoming more isolated and inactive.

　　有一個研究小組建立了一座行動實驗室，稱做「駕駛實驗室」，以了解年長的駕駛人面臨的挑戰，以及發現關鍵的壓力點在哪裡。研究顯示，放棄開車是年長者的健康和幸福衰退的重要原因之一，導致他們變得更加孤立、更加不活動。

　　* research〔ˈrisɜtʃ, rɪˈsɜtʃ〕*n.* 研究
　　mobile〔ˈmobl̩〕*adj.* 可動的；移動的
　　laboratory〔ˈlæbrə,torɪ〕*n.* 實驗室（= *lab*）
　　in order to V 為了　　challenge〔ˈtʃælɪndʒ〕*n.* 挑戰
　　discover〔dɪˈskʌvɚ〕*v.* 發現
　　key〔ki〕*adj.* 基本的；重要的；關鍵的
　　stress〔strɛs〕*n.* 壓力　　point〔pɔɪnt〕*n.* 點

give up 放棄　　decline〔dɪ'klaɪn〕*n.* 下降；衰退

well-being〔'wɛl'biɪŋ〕*n.* 幸福；健康；福祉

among〔ə'mʌŋ〕*prep.* 在…之中　　*lead to* 造成；導致

isolated〔'aɪsḷˌetɪd〕*adj.* 孤立的；隔離的

inactive〔ɪn'æktɪv〕*adj.* 不活動的

1. (**A**)　What is the purpose of the DriveLAB?

　　駕駛實驗室的目的是什麼？

　　(A) To find out older drivers' problems.

　　　　<u>找出年長駕駛人的問題。</u>

　　(B) To teach old people traffic rules.

　　　　教導年長者交通規則。

　　* purpose〔'pɝpəs〕*n.* 目的　　*find out* 發現；找出

　　rule〔rul〕*n.* 規則；規定

TEST 45 詳解

【2017 高考北京卷】

On a cold March day, a softball team was practicing.

Some girls were waiting for their next turns *at bat, stamping*

their feet to stay warm. *Suddenly*, one of the girls, *Paris*

White, fell to the ground. Her eyes rolled back. She started shaking. It was an emergency. She had suffered a sudden

heart failure. *Without immediate medical care*, she would die.

　　在一個寒冷的三月天裡，一支壘球隊正在練習。有些女孩在等候輪到自己打擊，她們跺著腳以保持溫暖。突然間其中一位女孩，芭莉絲·懷特倒在地上、翻白眼，並開始顫抖。發生了緊急情況，她是突發性的心臟衰竭。如果沒有立即的醫療處理，她就會死掉。

* softball〔'sɔft,bɔl〕*n.* 壘球　　practice〔'præktɪs〕*v.* 練習
　turn〔tɜn〕*n.* 輪流的順序　　bat〔bæt〕*n.* 打擊
　wait for** one's **turn at bat 等候輪到自己打擊
　stamp〔stæmp〕*v.* 跺；踏　　stay〔ste〕*v.* 保持
　suddenly〔'sʌdn̩lɪ〕*adv.* 突然地
　Paris White〔'pærɪs'hwaɪt〕*n.* 芭莉絲·懷特
　fall〔fɔl〕*v.* 跌倒　　ground〔graʊnd〕*n.* 地面
　roll〔rol〕*v.* 轉動　　shake〔ʃek〕*v.* 震動；顫抖
　emergency〔ɪ'mɜdʒənsɪ〕*n.* 緊急情況
　suffer〔'sʌfɚ〕*v.* 遭受；經歷　　sudden〔'sʌdn̩〕*adj.* 突然的
　failure〔'feljɚ〕*v.* 失敗；衰竭
　immediate〔ɪ'midɪɪt〕*adj.* 立即的；即刻的
　medical〔'mɛdɪkl̩〕*adj.* 醫療的　　care〔kɛr〕*n.* 治療

1. (**B**) What happened to Paris on a March day?
　　　芭莉絲在三月某天發生了什麼事？

　　(A) She caught a bad cold. 她得了重感冒。

　　(B) She had a sudden heart problem.

　　　　她突然出現了心臟問題。

　* happen〔'hæpən〕*v.* 發生

TEST 46

【2017 高考全國卷】

Gray wolves once were seen here and there in Yellowstone National Park and much of the U.S., but they were gradually displaced by human development. By the 1920s, wolves had practically disappeared from the Yellowstone area. They went farther north into the deep forests of Canada, where there were fewer humans around.

1. What does the underlined word "displaced" in the paragraph mean?

　　A. Forced out.

　　B. Tracked down.

TEST 47

【2017 高考浙江卷】

Italy is trying to control a growing immigrant population by demanding language skills in exchange for work permits, or in some cases, citizenship. In order to stay, an immigrant must take a test which requires him/her to write a postcard to an imaginary friend and answer a fictional job ad.

1. Why must an immigrant take a language test?

   A. To continue to stay in Italy.

   B. To teach his/her children Italian.

TEST 46 詳解

【2017 高考全國卷】

Gray wolves *once* were seen *here and there in Yellowstone*

National Park **and** *much of the U.S.*, **but** they were *gradually*

displaced *by human development.* *By the 1920s,* wolves had

practically disappeared *from the Yellowstone area.* They went

farther north into the deep forests of Canada, **where** *there were*

fewer humans around.

　　曾經有一度，在黃石國家公園和美國大部分地區，到處都看得到灰狼，但是它們因為人類的發展，而逐漸被驅離。到了 1920 年代，灰狼在黃石公園地區幾乎銷聲匿跡。牠們往更遠的北方遷移，進入加拿大的森林深處，在那裡人跡更罕至。

* gray〔gre〕*adj.* 灰色的（= *grey*）
  wolf〔wulf〕*n.* 狼【複數形為 wolves〔wulvz〕】
  once〔wʌns〕*adv.* 曾經；一度　　***here and there*** 到處
  Yellowstone National Park 美國黃石國家公園【位於美國西北部，主要位於美國懷俄明州（Wyoming〔waɪˈomɪŋ〕），部分位於蒙大拿州（Montana〔mɑnˈtænə〕）和愛達荷州（Idaho〔ˈaɪdəˌho〕），是美國第一座，也被認為是全世界第一座國家公園】
  gradually〔ˈgrædʒuəlɪ〕*adv.* 逐漸地
  displace〔dɪsˈples〕*v.* 強迫…離開

human (ˈhjumən) *adj.* 人類的　*n.* 人；人類
development (dɪˈvɛləpmənt) *n.* 發展；開發
practically (ˈpræktɪkl̩) *adv.* 實際上；幾乎
disappear (ˌdɪsəˈpɪr) *v.* 消失　　area (ˈɛrɪə) *n.* 地區；區域
farther (ˈfɑrðɚ) *adv.* 更遠地【是 far 的比較級】
north (nɔrθ) *adv.* 北方　　deep (dip) *adj.* 深的
forest (ˈfɔrɪst) *n.* 森林　　Canada (ˈkænədə) *n.* 加拿大
around (əˈraʊnd) *adv.* 在周圍；在四周

1. (**A**) What does the underlined word "displaced" in the
paragraph mean?
段落中畫底線的 displaced 這個字是什麼意思？

(A) Forced out. 被迫出去。

(B) Tracked down. 被追捕。

* underline (ˌʌndɚˈlaɪn) *v.* 畫底線
paragraph (ˈpærəˌgræf) *n.* 段落
mean (min) *v.* 意指；意謂　　force (fors) *v.* 強迫
track down 追蹤而查獲；追捕 (= *hunt down* = *find*)

TEST 47 詳解

【2017 高考浙江卷】

Italy is trying to control a growing immigrant population

by demanding language skills in exchange for work permits,

or *in some cases, citizenship.* *In order to stay*, an immigrant must take a test 〔*which* requires him/her to write a postcard to

an imaginary friend **and** answer a fictional job ad.〕

　　義大利試圖要控制越來越多的外來移民人口，要求他們要有語言技能，以交換工作許可，或是在某些情形中，公民權。為了要留下來，外來移民必須要參加一個考試，考試中要求他或她寫一封明信片，給一位想像中的朋友，還有回覆一個虛構的求職廣告。

* Italy〔'ɪtḷɪ〕*n.* 義大利　　control〔kən'trol〕*v.* 控制
growing〔'groɪŋ〕*adj.* 漸增的
immigrant〔'ɪməgrənt〕*adj.* 移入的　*n.* (移入的)移民
population〔ˌpɑpjə'leʃən〕*n.* 人口
demand〔dɪ'mænd〕*v.* 要求　　skill〔skɪl〕*n.* 技巧
exchange〔ɪks'tʃendʒ〕*n.* 交換　　*in exchange for* 與…交換
permit〔pɚ'mɪt〕*v.* 允許　　〔'pɝmɪt〕*n.* 許可證
case〔kes〕*n.* 情況；例子
citizenship〔'sɪtəzṇˌʃɪp〕*n.* 公民權
require〔rɪ'kwaɪr〕*v.* 需要；要求
postcard〔'postˌkɑrd〕*n.* 明信片
imaginary〔ɪ'mædʒəˌnɛrɪ〕*adj.* 想像的
fictional〔'fɪkʃənḷ〕*adj.* 虛構的　　ad〔æd〕*n.* 廣告

1. (**A**) Why must an immigrant take a language test?
外來移民為什麼必須參加語言測驗？

　(A) To continue to stay in Italy. 為了繼續留在義大利。

　(B) To teach his/her children Italian.
為了教他或她的小孩義大利語。

* continue〔kən'tɪnju〕*v.* 繼續
Italian〔ɪ'tæljən〕*n.* 義大利語

TEST 48

【2017 高考浙江卷】

Getting less sleep has become a bad habit for most American kids. According to a new survey by the National Sleep Foundation, 51% of kids aged 10 to 18 go to bed at 10 pm or later on school nights. Besides, nearly 60% of 7- to 12-year-olds said they felt tired during the day, and 15% said they had fallen asleep at school.

1. What is the new National Sleep Foundation survey on?

   A. American kids' sleeping habits.

   B. Teenagers' sleep-related diseases.

TEST 49

【2017 高考全國卷】

For many older people, particularly those living alone or in the country, driving is important for preserving their independence, giving them the freedom to get out and about without having to rely on others. But as people get older, they avoid any potentially challenging driving conditions and lose confidence in their driving skills. Finally they stop driving before they really need to.

1. Why is driving important for older people?

   A. It keeps them independent.

   B. It helps them save time.

TEST 48 詳解

【2017 高考浙江卷】

Getting less sleep has become a bad habit *for most American kids.* According to a new survey *by the National Sleep Foundation,* 51% of kids *aged 10 to 18* go to bed *at 10 pm or later on school nights.* Besides, nearly 60% of 7- to 12-year-olds said they felt tired *during the day,* **and** 15% said they had fallen asleep *at school.*

　　睡眠時間減少已經變成大部分美國小孩的壞習慣了。根據國家睡眠基金會所做的一項新調查，10 歲到 18 歲的小孩中，有百分之 51 在隔天要上學的晚上，10 點或更晚才睡覺。此外，7 歲到 12 歲的小孩中，有將近百分之 60 說他們白天會覺得疲倦，百分之 15 說他們在上課會睡著。

* habit〔ˈhæbɪt〕*n.* 習慣　　kid〔kɪd〕*n.* 小孩
　survey〔ˈsɜve〕*n.* 調查　　national〔ˈnæʃənl̩〕*adj.* 國家的
　foundation〔faʊnˈdeʃən〕*n.* 基金會
　aged〔edʒd〕*adj.* …歲的【後面接數字】
　go to bed 就寢；睡覺
　later〔ˈletə〕*adj.* 較晚的【late 的比較級】
　besides〔bɪˈsaɪdz〕*adv.* 此外
　nearly〔ˈnɪrlɪ〕*adv.* 將近；差不多

tired〔taɪrd〕*adj.* 疲倦的；疲乏的

during〔'dʊrɪŋ〕*prep.* 在⋯的期間　　***fall asleep*** 睡著

1.(**A**) What is the new National Sleep Foundation survey on?

國家睡眠基金會的新調查是關於什麼的？

 (A) American kids' sleeping habits.

 美國小孩的睡眠習慣。

 (B) Teenagers' sleep-related diseases.

 青少年與睡眠有關的疾病。

 * on〔ɑn〕*prep.* 關於

 teenager〔'tin,edʒɚ〕*n.* 十幾歲的青少年

 -related〔rɪ'letɪd〕*adj.* 與⋯有關的

 disease〔dɪ'ziz〕*n.* 疾病

TEST　49　詳解

【**2017 高考全國卷**】

For many older people, particularly those *living alone or*

in the country, driving is important for preserving their

independence, giving them the freedom *to get out **and*** about

without having to rely on others. ***But as*** *people get older,*

they avoid any *potentially* challenging driving conditions ***and*** lose confidence *in their driving skills. Finally* they stop

driving ***before*** *they really need to.*

對許多年長者，特別是獨居或住在鄉間的年長者，開車對於維持他們的獨立、給予他們外出的自由，以及不必依賴別人方面非常重要。但是隨著年紀增長，他們會避免任何可能有挑戰性的駕駛狀況，而對自己的駕駛技術失去信心。最後，他們在真正必要之前就不開車了。

* particularly〔pɚˈtɪkjələlɪ〕*adv.* 特別地；尤其
  alone〔əˈlon〕*adv.* 獨自；單獨地
  country〔ˈkʌntrɪ〕*n.* 鄉下
  preserve〔prɪˈzɝv〕*v.* 維持；保存
  independence〔ˌɪndɪˈpɛndəns〕*n.* 獨立
  freedom〔ˈfridəm〕*n.* 自由　　***get out*** 外出
  rely on 依賴（= *depend on*）　　avoid〔əˈvɔɪd〕*v.* 避免
  potentially〔pəˈtɛnʃəlɪ〕*adv.* 潛在地；可能地
  challenging〔ˈtʃælɪndʒɪŋ〕*adj.* 有挑戰性的；困難的
  condition〔kənˈdɪʃən〕*n.* 狀況；情形
  confidence〔ˈkɑnfədəns〕*n.* 自信　　skill〔skɪl〕*n.* 技巧

1. (**A**) Why is driving important for older people?

   開車對年長者而言為什麼很重要？

   (A) It keeps them independent. 它使他們保持獨立。

   (B) It helps them save time. 它幫助他們節省時間。

   * independent〔ˌɪndɪˈpɛndənt〕*adj.* 獨立的
     save〔sev〕*v.* 節省

TEST 50

【2017 高考全國卷】

The Last Picture Show was the last movie shown in the old theater. Though the movie is 30 years old, most of the 250 seats were filled with a teary-eyed audience wanting to say good-bye to the old building. The theater owner said he chose the movie because it seemed appropriate.

1. Why was *The Last Picture Show* put on?
   A. The audience requested it.
   B. The theater owner found it suitable.

TEST 50 詳解

【2017 高考全國卷】

The Last Picture Show was the last movie *shown in the old theater*. ***Though*** *the movie is 30 years old*, most of the 250 seats were filled with a teary-eyed audience *wanting to say good-bye to the old building*. The theater owner said he chose the movie ***because*** *it seemed appropriate*.

　　「最後一場電影」是這家舊電影院上映的最後一部電影。雖然這部電影已經 30 年了，但電影院裡 250 個座位，大多坐滿了淚眼汪汪的觀眾們，想要來向這棟老舊的建築物告別。電影院老闆說，他選擇了這部電影因為似乎挺合適的。

* theater〔ˈθiətɚ〕*n.* 劇院；電影院　　seat〔sit〕*n.* 座位；座椅
  be filled with 充滿　　teary-eyed〔ˈtɪrɪˌaɪd〕*adj.* 含著眼淚的
  audience〔ˈɔdɪəns〕*n.* 觀眾　　owner〔ˈonɚ〕*n.* 所有者
  appropriate〔əˈproprɪɪt〕*adj.* 適合的

1. (**B**) Why was *The Last Picture Show* put on?
   為什麼上演「最後一場電影」？
   (A) The audience requested it. 觀眾要求。
   (B) The theater owner found it suitable.
   　　戲院老闆覺得很適合。

   * ***put on*** 上演　　request〔rɪˈkwɛst〕*v.* 要求
     suitable〔ˈsutəbḷ〕*adj.* 適合的

TEST 51

【2017 高考全國卷】

The disappearance of gray wolves caused deer—a major food source for the wolf—to grow rapidly. Deer consumed large amounts of vegetation, which reduced plant diversity in the park. In the absence of wolves, coyote populations also grew quickly. The coyotes killed a large percentage of the park's red foxes, and completely drove away the park's beavers.

1. What did the disappearance of gray wolves bring about?

   A. Preservation of vegetation.

   B. Damage to local ecology.

TEST 51 詳解

【2017 高考全國卷】

The disappearance *of gray wolves* caused deer—*a major food source for the wolf*—to grow *rapidly*. Deer consumed large amounts of vegetation, ***which** reduced plant diversity in the park.* *In the absence of wolves,* coyote populations *also* grew *quickly*. The coyotes killed a large percentage of the park's red foxes, ***and** completely* drove away the park's beavers.

灰狼的消失導致鹿群的大量成長——鹿是狼的主要食物來源。鹿群吃掉了大量的植物，因而減少了公園裡的植物多樣性。在沒有狼群的時候，草原狼的總數也快速增加。草原狼咬死了公園裡大部分的紅狐，也將園區裡的河狸完全驅離。

* disappearance〔,dɪsə'pɪrəns〕*n.* 消失
  wolf〔wʊlf〕*n.* 狼【複數形為 wolves〔wʊlvz〕】
  deer〔dɪr〕*n.* 鹿【單複數同形】
  major〔'medʒɚ〕*adj.* 主要的　source〔sors〕*n.* 來源
  rapidly〔'ræpɪdlɪ〕*adv.* 迅速地
  consume〔kən'sum〕*v.* 消耗；吃（喝）

amount〔ə'maʊnt〕 *n.* 數量　　***large amounts of***　大量的

vegetation〔‚vɛdʒə'teʃən〕 *n.* 某地的植物【集合名詞，用單數】

reduce〔rɪ'djus〕 *v.* 減少

plant〔plænt〕 *n.* 植物

diversity〔də'vɜsətɪ〕 *n.* 多樣性

absence〔'æbsn̩s〕 *n.* 不在；缺席

in the absence of~　～不存在時

coyote

coyote〔kaɪ'ot , kaɪ'otɪ〕 *n.* (北美大草原的) 草原狼；郊狼

population〔‚pɑpjə'leʃən〕 *n.* 人口；(動植物的) 總數

percentage〔pɚ'sɛntɪdʒ〕 *n.* 百分比

fox〔fɑks〕 *n.* 狐狸

completely〔kəm'plitlɪ〕 *adv.* 完全地；徹底地

drive away　驅趕；驅離 (*= force away*)

beaver〔'bivɚ〕 *n.* 河狸

beaver

1. (**B**) What did the disappearance of
gray wolves bring about?
灰狼的消失造成了什麼？

(A) Preservation of vegetation.　植物的保存。

(B) Damage to local ecology.　<u>當地生態受損。</u>

* ***bring about***　造成；招致

　　preservation〔‚prɛzɚ'veʃən〕 *n.* 保存

　　damage〔'dæmɪdʒ〕 *n.* 損害；損失

　　local〔'lokl̩〕 *adj.* 當地的；本地的

　　ecology〔ɪ'kɑlədʒɪ〕 *n.* 生態 (學)

TEST 52

【2017 高考浙江卷】

Mr. Williams, a well-known painter, was impressed with Benjamin and gave him two books. The books were long and dull, so Benjamin could only read a little. But he later said, "Those two books were my companions by day, and under my pillow at night." Though he probably understood very little of the books, they were his introduction to classical paintings. The nine-year-old boy decided then that he would be an artist.

1. Mr. Williams' two books helped Benjamin to
   A. master the use of paints.
   B. make up his mind to be a painter.

TEST 53

【2017 高考浙江卷】

"More children are going to bed with TVs on, and there are more opportunities to stay awake, with more homework, the Internet and the phone," says a sleep researcher. She says these activities at bedtime can get kids all excited and make it hard for them to calm down and sleep.

1. Why do teenagers go to sleep late according to the researcher?
   A. They tend to do things that excite them.
   B. They don't need to go to school early.

TEST 52 詳解

【2017 高考浙江卷】

Mr. Williams, *a well-known painter*, was impressed with
同 位 語

Benjamin *and* gave him two books. The books were long and

dull, *so* Benjamin could *only* read a little. *But* he *later* said,

"Those two books were my companions *by day*, *and* under my

pillow at night." [*Though* he probably understood very little

the of books,] they were his introduction *to classical paintings*.

The nine-year-old boy decided *then that* he would be an artist.

威廉斯先生是一位名畫家,他對班哲明印象很深刻,所以送給他兩
本書。這兩本書很長很乏味,所以班哲明只能看懂一點點。但是他後來
說:「那兩本書白天是我的同伴,晚上就放在我的枕頭底下。」這兩本
書雖然他懂得很少,但卻是他進入古典繪畫的入門。這名九歲大的男孩
那時就決定了,未來要當畫家。

> * Williams〔'wɪljəmz〕*n.* 威廉斯【姓氏名】
> well-known〔'wɛl'non〕*adj.* 著名的
> painter〔'pentɚ〕*n.* 畫家
> impressed〔ɪm'prɛst〕*adj.* 印象深刻的
> Benjamin〔'bɛndʒəmən〕*n.* 班哲明【男子名】
> dull〔dʌl〕*adj.* 乏味的;單調的

later〔'letɚ〕*adv.* 後來；稍後

companion〔kəm'pænjən〕*n.* 同伴；夥伴

under〔'ʌndɚ〕*prep.* 在…之下　　pillow〔'pɪlo〕*n.* 枕頭

probably〔'prɑbəblɪ〕*adv.* 可能

introduction〔͵ɪntrə'dʌkʃən〕*n.* 介紹；入門 < *to* >

classical〔'klæsɪkḷ〕*adj.* 古典的

painting〔'pentɪŋ〕*n.* 繪畫；畫作

artist〔'ɑrtɪst〕*n.* 藝術家；畫家

1.(**B**)　Mr. Williams' two books helped Benjamin to
威廉斯先生的兩本書幫助班哲明

(A) master the use of paints. 精通顏料的使用。

(B) make up his mind to be a painter.
下定決心成為畫家。

* master〔'mæstɚ〕*v.* 精通；熟練
paint〔pent〕*n.* 油漆；顏料
make up *one's **mind*** 下定決心

TEST 53 詳解

【2017 高考浙江卷】

"More children are going to bed *with TVs on*, **and** there

are more opportunities to stay awake, *with more homework*,

the Internet and the phone," says a sleep researcher. She says

these activities *at bedtime* can get <u>kids</u> *all excited* **and** make ***it***
　　　　　　　　　　　　　　　　受　　受補　　　　　虛受詞

hard [*for them to calm down and sleep.*]
受補　　　　　眞正受詞

　　一位研究睡眠的專家說：「更多小孩去睡覺時電視機還開著，而且保持醒著的機會增加了，因爲有更多的家庭作業、網際網路和手機。」她說這些就寢時間的活動可能會使孩子變得很興奮，使得他們要平靜下來睡覺很困難。

* opportunity〔͵ɑpɚ'tunətɪ〕*n.* 機會
  stay〔ste〕*v.* 保持　　awake〔ə'wek〕*adj.* 醒著的
  homework〔'hom͵wɝk〕*n.* 家庭作業
  Internet〔'ɪntɚ͵nɛt〕*n.* 網際網路
  researcher〔ri'sɝtʃɚ〕*n.* 研究人員
  activity〔æk'tɪvətɪ〕*n.* 活動
  bedtime〔'bɛd͵taɪm〕*n.* 就寢時間
  excited〔ɪk'saɪtɪd〕*adj.* 興奮的
  calm〔kɑm〕*v.* 平靜；鎮定 < *down* >

1. (**A**) Why do teenagers go to sleep late according to the researcher? 根據研究人員所說，爲什麼青少年很晚睡覺？
   (A) They tend to do things that excite them.
   　　<u>他們通常會做一些使他們興奮的事情。</u>
   (B) They don't need to go to school early.
   　　他們不必很早去上學。

   * teenager〔'tin͵edʒɚ〕*n.* 十幾歲的青少年
     tend to V 傾向於；通常

TEST 54

【2017 高考江蘇卷】

Chewang Norphel, known as the Ice Man, lives in a mountainous region in India. The loss of glacier due to global warming represents an enormous threat to agriculture. Without the glaciers, water will arrive in the rivers at times when it can damage crops. His inspiration came from seeing the waste of water over winter. He directed the wasted water into shallow basins where it froze and was stored until spring. His fields of ice supply perfectly timed irrigation water.

1. What did the Ice Man do to reduce the effect of global warming?

   A. Store ice for future use.

   B. Change the irrigation time.

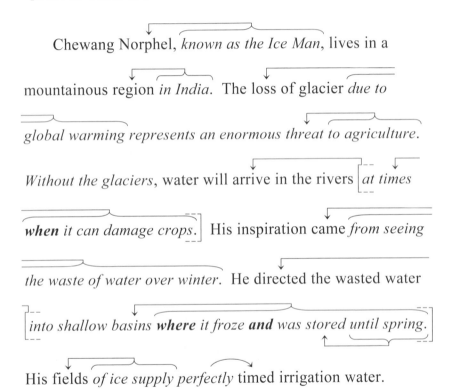

TEST 54 詳解

【2017 高考江蘇卷】

Chewang Norphel, *known as the Ice Man*, lives in a mountainous region *in India*. The loss of glacier *due to global warming represents an enormous threat to agriculture.* *Without the glaciers*, water will arrive in the rivers *at times when it can damage crops.* His inspiration came *from seeing the waste of water over winter.* He directed the wasted water *into shallow basins where it froze and was stored until spring.* His fields *of ice supply perfectly* timed irrigation water.

　　車旺‧諾菲爾被稱爲「冰人」，他住在印度的一處山區。由於全球暖化所造成的冰河消失，意味著對農業重大的威脅。沒有冰河，雪水灌入河流時，會造成農作物受損。看到冬天時浪費水的情況給了他靈感。他把浪費掉的水導向較淺的盆地，在那裡水結成冰，貯藏起來直到春天來臨。他的冰田完美地配合灌漑用水的時間。

　　* Chewang Norphel〔tʃəˋwɑŋ ˋnɔrfɛl〕*n.* 車旺‧諾菲爾【人名】
　　be known as 被稱爲　　ice〔aɪs〕*n.* 冰

mountainous〔'maʊntn̩əs〕*adj.* 山地的

region〔'ridʒən〕*n.* 地區　　India〔'ɪndɪə〕*n.* 印度

loss〔lɔs〕*n.* 喪失；遺失　　glacier〔'gleʃɚ〕*n.* 冰河

due to 因為；由於 (= *because of*)

global〔'globl̩〕*adj.* 全球的　　***global warming*** 全球暖化

represent〔ˌrɛprɪ'zɛnt〕*v.* 意味；表示

enormous〔ɪ'nɔrməs〕*adj.* 巨大的　　threat〔θrɛt〕*n.* 威脅

agriculture〔'ægrɪˌkʌltʃɚ〕*n.* 農業

damage〔'dæmɪdʒ〕*v.* 損害；損傷　　crop〔krɑp〕*n.* 農作物

inspiration〔ˌɪnspə'reʃən〕*n.* 靈感；啟示

waste〔west〕*n., v.* 浪費

direct〔də'rɛkt〕*v.* 使朝向　　shallow〔'ʃælo〕*adj.* 淺的

basin〔'besn̩〕*n.* 盆地　　freeze〔friz〕*v.* 結冰

store〔stor〕*v.* 貯藏；儲存　　field〔fild〕*n.* 田野

supply〔sə'plaɪ〕*n.* 供給；供應

perfectly〔'pɝfɪktlɪ〕*adv.* 完全地；完美地

time〔taɪm〕*v.* 配合時機

irrigation〔ˌɪrə'geʃən〕*n.* 灌溉

1. (**A**) What did the Ice Man do to reduce the effect of global
    warming? 冰人為了減少全球暖化的影響做了什麼？

    (A) Store ice for future use. 貯藏冰做未來使用。

    (B) Change the irrigation time. 改變灌溉時間。

    * reduce〔rɪ'djus〕*v.* 減少；減輕
      effect〔ɪ'fɛkt〕*n.* 結果；影響
      future〔'fjutʃɚ〕*adj.* 未來的
      change〔tʃendʒ〕*v.* 改變

TEST 55

【2017 高考天津卷】

Do you know we spend a large part of our lives waiting? The purest form of waiting is the Watched-Pot Wait. It is absolutely annoying. Take filling up the kitchen sink as an example. One can do nothing but keep both eyes fixed on the sink until it's full. During these waits, the brain slips away and wanders about. This kind of wait makes the waiter helpless and mindless.

1. While doing a Watched-Pot Wait, we tend to

   A. get absent-minded.

   B. stay focused.

TEST 55 詳解

【2017 高考天津卷】

Do you know we spend a large part of our lives waiting?

The purest form *of waiting* is the Watched-Pot Wait. It is

absolutely annoying. Take filling up the kitchen sink as an
　　　　　　　　　　　　　　　　　　　　　　受詞

example. One can do nothing ***but*** keep both eyes *fixed on the*
　　　　　　　　　　　　　　　　　　　　　　　受　　　　受　補

*sink **until** it's full. During these waits*, the brain slips away

and wanders about. This kind of wait makes the waiter
　　　　　　　　　　　　　　　　　　　　　　　　　　受

helpless and mindless.
　受　補

　　你知道我們的生活中，有一大部分的時間在等待嗎？最純粹的等待
就是「乾等」。這完全就是煩人。以在廚房水槽裝滿水為例。除了兩眼
固定在水槽那裡，直到水裝滿之外，什麼也不能做。在這種等待時，大
腦就溜出去神遊了。這種等待會讓等候者很無助，也不用腦筋。

* 人 + spend + 時 + V-ing　某人花費時間做某事
  pure〔pjʊr〕*adj.* 純粹的　　form〔fɔrm〕*n.* 形式
  pot〔pɑt〕*n.* 壺【watched-pot 的用法來自諺語：A watched
  　pot never boils. 苦候水不沸；急不得。】

absolutely〔'æbsə,lutlɪ〕*adv.* 絕對地；完全地

annoying〔ə'nɔɪɪŋ〕*adj.* 令人困擾的；煩人的

Take ~ as an example. 以～為例。(= *Take ~ for example.*)

fill up 裝滿　　sink〔sɪŋk〕*n.* 水槽

do nothing but V 除了～外什麼也不能做；只能 (= *only*)

fix〔fɪks〕*v.* 固定　　full〔fʊl〕*adj.* 滿的

during〔'dʊrɪŋ〕*prep.* 在…的期間

brain〔bren〕*n.* 頭腦　　slip〔slɪp〕*v.* 溜走 < *away* >

wander〔'wɑndɚ〕*v.* 徘徊；到處走

about〔ə'baʊt〕*adv.* 到處

waiter〔'wetɚ〕*n.* 等候者

helpless〔'hɛlplɪs〕*adj.* 無助的

mindless〔'maɪndlɪs〕*adj.* 無知的；不用腦筋的

1. (**A**) While doing a Watched-Pot Wait, we tend to

　　當我們在「乾等」的時候，我們通常會

　　(A) get absent-minded. 變得心不在焉。

　　(B) stay focused. 保持專注。

　　* while〔hwaɪl〕*conj.* 當…的時候

　　　tend to V 傾向於；通常

　　　absent-minded〔'æbsn̩t,maɪndɪd〕*adj.* 心不在焉的

　　　stay〔ste〕*v.* 保持

　　　focused〔'fokəst〕*adj.* 專注的

TEST 56

【 2017 高考江蘇卷 】

Floods have become more damaging in Bangladesh. Mohammed Rezwan saw opportunity where others saw only disaster. His organization runs 100 rivers boats that serve as floating libraries, schools, and health clinics, and are equipped with solar panels and other communicating facilities. They create floating connectivity to replace flooded roads and highways. They show people how to make floating gardens and fish ponds to prevent starvation during the wet season.

1. What is special with regard to Rezwan's project?

   A. His organization makes the best of a bad situation.

   B. He provides ferry boat transportation in Bangladesh.

TEST 56 詳解

【2017 高考江蘇卷】

Floods have become more damaging *in Bangladesh.*
Mohammed Rezwan saw opportunity *where others saw only*
disaster. His organization runs 100 rivers boats *that serve as*
*floating libraries, schools, **and** health clinics, **and** are equipped*
*with solar panels **and** other communicating facilities.* They
create floating connectivity *to replace flooded roads **and***
highways. They show people ***how** to make floating gardens*
***and** fish ponds to prevent starvation during the wet season.*

在孟加拉，洪水已經變得更加具有破壞力。在別人只有看到災難的地方，穆罕默德・瑞茲萬看到了機會。他的組織經營 100 艘內河船，用來當作浮動圖書館、學校和保健診所，上面裝備有太陽能面板和其他通訊設備。他們創造了浮動連線，來取代被淹沒的街道和幹道。他們教人如何築出浮動的菜園和魚池，以防止雨季時挨餓。

* flood〔flʌd〕*n.* 洪水；水災　*v.* 淹水；淹沒
  damaging〔ˈdæmɪdʒɪŋ〕*adj.* 造成損害的；有破壞力的
  Bangladesh〔͵bæŋgləˈdɛʃ〕*n.* 孟加拉
  Mohammed Rezwan〔moˈhæmɪd ˈrɛzwən〕
  　n. 穆罕默德・瑞茲萬【人名】
  opportunity〔͵ɑpɚˈtjunətɪ〕*n.* 機會

disaster〔dɪzˋæstə〕*n.* 災害；不幸

organization〔͵ɔrgənəˋzeʃən〕*n.* 組織　　run〔rʌn〕*v.* 經營

river boat 內河船　　*serve as* 充當；當作

floating〔ˋflotɪŋ〕*adj.* 流動的；浮動的

clinic〔ˋklɪnɪk〕*n.* 診所　　equip〔ɪˋkwɪp〕*v.* 使裝備＜*with*＞

solar〔ˋsolə〕*adj.* 太陽（能）的　　panel〔ˋpænl̩〕*n.* 鑲板；面板

communicate〔kəˋmjunə͵ket〕*v.* 傳達；通訊

facility〔fəˋsɪlətɪ〕*n.* 設施；設備　　create〔krɪˋet〕*v.* 創造

connectivity〔͵kanɛkˋtɪvətɪ〕*n.* 連接；連線

replace〔rɪˋples〕*v.* 代替；取代

highway〔ˋhaɪ͵we〕*n.* 公路；幹道

garden〔ˋgɑrdn̩〕*n.* 花園；果園；菜園

pond〔pɑnd〕*n.* 池塘　　prevent〔prɪˋvɛnt〕*v.* 預防；防止

starvation〔stɑrˋveʃən〕*n.* 飢荒；飢餓

during〔ˋdʊrɪŋ〕*prep.* 在…的期間

wet〔wɛt〕*adj.* 濕的；潮濕的　　*wet season* 濕季；雨季

1. (**A**) What is special with regard to Rezwan's project?

　　關於瑞茲萬的計畫有什麼特別的？

　　(A) His organization makes the best of a bad situation.

　　　　他的組織能善用非常不好的情況。

　　(B) He provides ferry boat transportation in Bangladesh.

　　　　他提供孟加拉的渡輪運輸。

　　＊ special〔ˋspɛʃəl〕*adj.* 特別的

　　　 regard〔rɪˋgɑrd〕*n.* 顧慮；關心　　*with regard to* 關於…

　　　 project〔ˋprɑdʒɛkt〕*n.* 計畫；企畫

　　　 situation〔͵sɪtʃuˋeʃən〕*n.* 情況；狀態

　　　 make the best of a bad situation 善處逆境；善用不好的情況

　　　 provide〔prəˋvaɪd〕*v.* 提供　　ferry〔ˋfɛrɪ〕*n.* 渡船

　　　 transportation〔͵trænspəˋteʃən〕*n.* 運輸；交通工具

TEST 57

【2017 高考天津卷】

I once took a vacation in Italy. Looking at a fantastic view of the blue sea, white buildings and green trees, I paused to catch my breath and then positioned myself to take the best photo. Unfortunately, just as I took out my camera, a woman approached, and stood right in front of my view. Like me, this woman was here to stop, sigh, and appreciate the view.

1. What happened when the author was about to take a photo?

A. A woman blocked her view.

B. A friend approached from behind.

TEST 58

【2016 高考全國卷】

I am a stem cell deliveryman. I have 42 hours to carry stem cells in my little box because I've got two ice packs and that's how long they last. From the time the stem cells are harvested from a donor to the time they can be implanted in the patient, we've got 72 hours at most. So I am always conscious of time.

1. Why does the man have to complete his trip within 42 hours?

   A. The operation needs that much time.

   B. The ice won't last any longer.

TEST 57 詳解

【2017 高考天津卷】

I *once* took a vacation *in Italy.* *Looking at a fantastic view of the blue sea, white buildings **and** green trees,* I paused to catch my breath **and** *then* positioned myself *to take the best photo.* *Unfortunately, just **as** I took out my camera,* a woman approached, **and** stood *right in front of my view.* *Like me,* this woman was here to stop, sigh, **and** appreciate the view.

有一次我到義大利度假。看著藍色的大海、白色的建築，和綠色樹林的絕佳美景，我停下來休息一下，然後站定一個適當位置，想拍出最棒的照片。不幸的是，正當我拿出相機時，有一位女士走近，就站在我的視線前面。就像我一樣，這位女士也在這裡駐足、讚嘆、欣賞美景。

* once〔wʌns〕*adv.* 曾經；有一次
  vacation〔veˈkeʃən〕*n.* 假期　　Italy〔ˈɪtḷɪ〕*n.* 義大利
  fantastic〔fænˈtæstɪk〕*adj.* 極好的；很棒的
  view〔vju〕*n.* 景色；視線　　pause〔pɔz〕*v.* 暫停
  breath〔brɛθ〕*n.* 呼吸
  catch** one's **breath 喘口氣；休息一下
  position〔pəˈzɪʃən〕*v.* 把～放在適當位置
  photo〔ˈfoto〕*n.* 照片
  unfortunately〔ʌnˈfɔrtʃənɪtlɪ〕*adv.* 不幸地；遺憾地

take out 拿出　　camera〔ˋkæmərə〕*n.* 照相機

approach〔əˋprotʃ〕*v.* 接近　　*in front of* 在～前面

sigh〔saɪ〕*v.* 嘆息；驚嘆　　appreciate〔əˋpriʃɪ͵et〕*v.* 欣賞

1.(**A**) What happened when the author was about to take a
photo? 當作者正要拍照時，發生了什麼事？

(A) A woman blocked her view.

<u>一位女士擋住她的視線。</u>

(B) A friend approached from behind.

一位朋友從後面接近。

* happen〔ˋhæpən〕*v.* 發生　　author〔ˋɔθɚ〕*n.* 作者

be about to V 正要；即將　　block〔blɑk〕*v.* 阻擋

from behind 從後面

TEST 58 詳解

【2016 高考全國卷】

I am a stem cell deliveryman. I have 42 hours *to carry*

*stem cells in my little box **because** I've got two ice packs **and***

*that's **how** long they last. From the time the stem cells are*

harvested from a donor to the time they can be implanted in the patient, we've got 72 hours *at most*. So I am *always*

conscious of time.

　　我是一個幹細胞送貨員。要運送我的小箱子裡的幹細胞，我有 42 小時的時間，因為我有兩個冰袋，那就是冰袋能維持的時間。從捐贈者那裡獲取幹細胞開始，到它們被植入病人的體內，我們最多只有 72 小時。所以，我總是隨時在注意時間。

> * stem〔stɛm〕*n.* 莖；柄　　cell〔sɛl〕*n.* 細胞
> **stem cell** 幹細胞【幹細胞能在短時間內修復各種器官組織，被應用在治療技術方面，療效極佳】
> deliveryman〔dɪˈlɪvərɪmən〕*n.* 送貨員
> pack〔pæk〕*n.* 一包；一袋　　**ice pack** 冰袋
> last〔læst〕*v.* 持續　　harvest〔ˈhɑrvɪst〕*v.* 收穫；獲得
> donor〔ˈdonɚ〕*n.* 捐贈者
> implant〔ɪmˈplænt〕*v.* 植入；注入
> patient〔ˈpeʃənt〕*n.* 病人；患者　　**at most** 最多；頂多
> conscious〔ˈkɑnʃəs〕*adj.* 有意識的；察覺的 < *of* >

1. (**B**) Why does the man have to complete his trip within 42 hours? 為什麼這位男士必須在 42 小時內完成他的行程？

　　(A) The operation needs that much time.
　　　　手術需要那麼多的時間。

　　(B) The ice won't last any longer. 冰無法持續更久。

> * complete〔kəmˈplit〕*v.* 完成
> trip〔trɪp〕*n.* 旅行；一趟行程
> within〔wɪðˈɪn〕*prep.* 在…以內
> operation〔ˌɑpəˈreʃən〕*n.* 手術；操作

TEST 59

【2016 高考全國卷】

The meaning of silence varies from culture to culture. Silences may be thoughtful, or they may be empty when a person has nothing to say. Silence may be viewed by some cultural groups as extremely uncomfortable. However, it is valued and seen as necessary for understanding a person's needs in other cultural groups.

1. What does the author say about silence in conversation?

　A. It is culture-specific.

　B. It is content-based.

TEST 60

【2016 高考全國卷】

Anyone who has ever been helped by a social worker has Jane Addams to thank. Addams helped the poor and worked for peace. She encouraged a sense of community by creating shelters and promoting education and services for people in need. In 1931, Addams became the first American woman to win the Nobel Peace Prize.

1. What is Jane Addams noted for in history?
   A. Her social work.
   B. Her efforts to win a prize.

TEST 59 詳解

【2016 高考全國卷】

The meaning *of silence* varies *from culture to culture.*

Silences may be thoughtful, *or* they may be empty *when a*

person has nothing to say. Silence may be viewed *by some*

cultural groups as *extremely* uncomfortable. *However*, it is

valued *and* seen as necessary *for understanding a person's*

needs in other cultural groups.

　　沈默的意義每個文化都不同。沈默可能很體貼，又或者在一個人無
話可說時，沈默可能很無聊。有些文化團體可能認為沈默令人非常不舒
服，然而，在有些文化團體裡，沈默是受到重視的，而且要了解一個人
的需求，沈默被視為是必要的。

* meaning〔'minɪŋ〕*n.* 意思；意義　　silence〔'saɪləns〕*n.* 沈默
vary〔'vɛrɪ〕*v.* 變化；不同（= *differ*）
culture〔'kʌltʃə〕*n.* 文化
vary*/*differ from A to A 每個 A 都不同
thoughtful〔'θɔtfəl〕*adj.* 沈思的；體貼的
empty〔'ɛmptɪ〕*adj.* 空虛的；無聊的
view A as B 視 A 為 B（= *see A as B*）
cultural〔'kʌltʃərəl〕*adj.* 文化的

extremely〔ɪk'strimlɪ〕*adv.* 極端地；非常地
uncomfortable〔ʌn'kʌmfətəbḷ〕*adj.* 不舒服的
value〔'vælju〕*v.* 重視
necessary〔'nɛsə,sɛrɪ〕*adj.* 必要的；必需的

1. (**A**) What does the author say about silence in conversation?
關於對話中的沈默，作者說了什麼？

　(A) It is culture-specific. 它與文化密切相關。

　(B) It is content-based. 它以內容為基礎。

　*author〔'ɔθɚ〕*n.* 作者
　conversation〔,kɑnvɚ'seʃən〕*n.* 會話；談話
　specific〔spɪ'sɪfɪk〕*adj.* 特定的
　culture-specific　*adj.* 有文化特性的；與文化密切相關的
　content-based〔'kɑntɛnt,best〕*adj.* 以內容為基礎的

TEST 60 詳解

【2016 高考全國卷】

Anyone ***who has ever been helped by a social worker*** has

Jane Addams to thank. Addams helped the poor ***and*** worked

for peace. She encouraged a sense of community *by creating*

*shelters **and** promoting education **and** services for people in* *need.* ⌐ *In 1931*, Addams became the first American woman

to win the Nobel Peace Prize.

　　任何曾經受過社工幫助的人都應該感謝珍・亞當斯。亞當斯幫助窮人，爲和平而努力。她藉由建立庇護所，倡導給窮人的教育和服務，促進社區歸屬感。在 1931 年，亞當斯成爲第一位獲得諾貝爾和平獎的美國女性。

　　* social〔'soʃəl〕*adj.* 社會的
　　social worker 社工；社會福利工作者
　　Jane Addams〔dʒen 'ædəmz〕*n.* 珍・亞當斯【1860-1935，是美國
　　　　社會工作者、社會學家和哲學家。她因爭取婦女、黑人移居的權利而獲
　　　　得 1931 年諾貝爾和平獎，也是美國第一個贏得諾貝爾和平獎的女性】
　　have *sb.* ***to thank*** 應該責怪或感謝某人
　　poor〔pur〕*adj.* 貧窮的；窮困的　　***the poor*** 窮人；貧民
　　peace〔pis〕*n.* 和平　　encourage〔ɪn'kɝɪdʒ〕*v.* 鼓勵；刺激
　　sense〔sɛns〕*n.* 感覺　　community〔kə'mjunətɪ〕*n.* 社區
　　create〔krɪ'et〕*v.* 創造　　shelter〔'ʃɛltɚ〕*n.* 庇護所；避難所
　　promote〔prə'mot〕*v.* 促進；提倡
　　education〔,ɛdʒə'keʃən〕*n.* 教育　　service〔'sɝvɪs〕*n.* 服務
　　in need 有需要；窮困　　win〔wɪn〕*v.* 贏得
　　prize〔praɪz〕*n.* 獎　　***Nobel Peace Prize*** 諾貝爾和平獎

1.(**A**)　What is Jane Addams noted for in history?
　　　珍・亞當斯在歷史上以什麼有名？
　　　(A) Her social work. 她的社會工作。
　　　(B) Her efforts to win a prize. 她得獎的努力。

　　　* noted〔'notɪd〕*adj.* 有名的（= *famous*）
　　　history〔'hɪstrɪ〕*n.* 歷史　　effort〔'ɛfɚt〕*n.* 努力

TEST 61

【2016 高考江蘇卷】

El Niño, a Spanish term for "the Christ Child," was used by South American fishermen to name a global weather pattern which happens every two to seven years and reduces the amount of fish caught around Christmas. El Niño sees warmer water, collected over several years in the western Pacific, flow back eastwards when winds that normally blow westwards weaken.

1. What can we learn about El Niño from the paragraph?

   A. It is named after a South American fisherman.

   B. It involves a change in the direction of the water flow in the ocean.

TEST 61 詳解

【2016 高考江蘇卷】

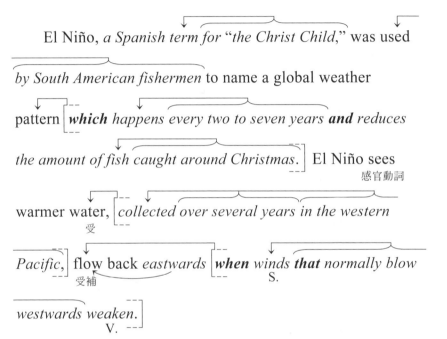

El Niño (聖嬰現象)是西班牙語,這個名詞指「聖嬰」,南美洲的漁夫用來指一種全球的天氣型態,每隔二到七年發生一次,大約在聖誕節的時候,此時漁獲量會減少。聖嬰現象發生時,數年來累積在西太平洋的溫暖海水,會向東回流,而通常向西吹的風會減弱。

* El Niño〔ɛl'ninjo〕n. 聖嬰現象【指嚴重影響全球氣候的太平洋熱帶海域的大風及海水的大規模移動】

Spanish〔'spænɪʃ〕adj. 西班牙(人、語)的

term〔tɝm〕n. 名詞　　Christ〔kraɪst〕n. 基督

Christ Child 聖嬰【又可稱為 Baby Jesus、Divine Infant,或 the Holy Child 等,指從出生到 12 歲的耶穌基督】

South American 南美洲的　　fisherman〔ˈfɪʃəmən〕*n.* 漁夫
global〔ˈglobl̩〕*adj.* 全球的　　weather〔ˈwɛðɚ〕*n.* 天氣
pattern〔ˈpætən〕*n.* 型態；模式
happen〔ˈhæpən〕*v.* 發生　　reduce〔rɪˈdjus〕*v.* 減少
amount〔əˈmaʊnt〕*n.* 數量　　fish〔fɪʃ〕*n.* 魚【單複數同形】
around〔əˈraʊnd〕*prep.* 大約；差不多
Christmas〔ˈkrɪsməs〕*n.* 聖誕節
collect〔kəˈlɛkt〕*v.* 收集；聚集
several〔ˈsɛvərəl〕*adj.* 數個　　western〔ˈwɛstən〕*adj.* 西方的
Pacific〔pəˈsɪfɪk〕*n.* 太平洋　　flow〔flo〕*v., n.* 流動
eastwards〔ˈistwɚdz〕*adv.* 向東方
normally〔ˈnɔrml̩ɪ〕*adv.* 正常地；通常
blow〔blo〕*v.*（風）吹
westwards〔ˈwɛstwɚdz〕*adv.* 向西方
weaken〔ˈwikən〕*v.* 減弱

1.（ **B** ）What can we learn about El Niño from the paragraph?
關於聖嬰現象，從這一段我們得知什麼？

(A) It is named after a South American fisherman.
它是以一名南美洲的漁夫來命名的。

(B) It involves a change in the direction of the water
flow in the ocean. 它與海洋中水流方向的改變有關。

* learn〔lɝn〕*v.* 學習；得知
paragraph〔ˈpærəˌgræf〕*n.* 段落
be named after 以～被命名
involve〔ɪnˈvɑlv〕*v.* 涉及；與～有關
change〔tʃendʒ〕*n.* 改變
direction〔dəˈrɛkʃən〕*n.* 方向　　ocean〔ˈoʃən〕*n.* 海洋

TEST 62

【2016 高考北京卷】

California condors are North America's largest birds. However, electrical lines have been killing them off. At night they can't see the power lines. Their wings can bridge the gap between lines, resulting in electrocution. So scientists used tall poles, placed in large training areas, to teach the birds to stay clear of electrical lines by giving them a painful but not deadly electric shock. Now their death rate has dropped from 66% to 18%.

1. Researchers have found electrical lines are _____.

　A. big killers of California condors

　B. rest places for condors at night

TEST 62 詳解

【2016 高考北京卷】

California condors are North America's largest birds. However, electrical lines have been killing them off. *At night they can't see the power lines.* Their wings can bridge the gap *between lines, resulting in electrocution.* *So* scientists used tall poles, *placed in large training areas,* to teach the birds to stay clear of electrical lines *by giving them a painful* ***but*** *not deadly electric shock.* *Now* their death rate has dropped *from 66% to 18%.*

加州神鷹是北美洲最大的鳥。然而，高壓電纜線逐漸使牠們滅絕。晚上牠們看不到電線。牠們的翅膀展開可以超過電纜線之間的間隔，而造成觸電。所以，科學家們使用很高的竿子，放置在大型訓練場裡，藉由給牠們一點點痛苦但不會致命的電擊，教導牠們遠離電纜線。現在，牠們的死亡率已經下降，從百分之 66 降到了百分之 18。

* California〔͵kælə'fɔrnjə〕 *n.* 加州【位於美國西部太平洋沿岸，首都沙加緬度（Sacramento〔͵sækrə'mɛnto〕）】

condor〔'kandɚ〕 *n.* 大兀鷹 ***California condor*** 加州神鷹

electrical〔ɪ'lɛktrɪkḷ〕*adj.* 電氣的　　line〔laɪn〕*n.* 線

electrical line 電線　　***kill off*** 滅絕；毀滅

power〔'pauɚ〕*n.* 電力　　wing〔wɪŋ〕*n.* 翼；翅膀

bridge〔brɪdʒ〕*v.* 架橋於；填補（空隙等）

gap〔gæp〕*n.* 縫隙；缺口；間隔

result in 導致；造成（ *= lead to = cause* ）

electrocution〔ɪ,lɛktrə'kjuʃən〕*n.* 觸電死亡

pole〔pol〕*n.* 柱子；竿

place〔ples〕*v.* 放置；安裝（ *= put* ）　　*n.* 場所；地點

training〔'trenɪŋ〕*n.* 訓練　　area〔'ɛrɪə〕*n.* 地區；區域

stay clear of 避開（ *= stay away from* ）

painful〔'penfəl〕*adj.* 痛苦的　　deadly〔'dɛdlɪ〕*adj.* 致命的

electric〔ɪ'lɛktrɪk〕*adj.* 電的　　shock〔ʃɑk〕*n.* 電擊；觸電

electric shock 電擊；觸電　　rate〔ret〕*n.* 率；比率

death rate 死亡率　　drop〔drɑp〕*v.* 降低；減少

1. (**A**) Researchers have found electrical lines are _____.

　　研究人員發現電線是 _____。

　　(A) big killers of California condors

　　　　加州神鷲的大殺手

　　(B) rest places for condors at night

　　　　加州神鷲晚上的休息地

　　* researcher〔ri'sɝtʃɚ〕*n.* 研究人員

　　　killer〔'kɪlɚ〕*n.* 殺手　　rest〔rɛst〕*n.* 休息

TEST 63

【2016 高考全國卷】

Ms. Garza had been living in Brownsville, Texas, and never planned to move away. Even when her son asked her to move to San Antonio to help with his children, she politely refused. After a year of friendly discussion, she finally said yes. Today all three generations regard the move as a success because it gives them a closer relationship than they would have had in separate cities.

1. Why was Garza's move a success?
   A. It strengthened her family ties.
   B. It improved her living conditions.

TEST 63 詳解

【2016 高考全國卷】

Ms. Garza had been living *in Brownsville, Texas*, ***and***

never planned to move away. *Even **when** her son asked her*

to move to San Antonio to help with his children, she *politely*

refused. *After a year of friendly discussion*, she *finally* said

yes. *Today* all three generations regard the move as a success

***because** it gives them a closer relationship **than** they would*

have had in separate cities.

　　加爾札女士一直住在德州的布朗斯維爾市，從沒有計畫要搬走。即使是當她兒子請她搬到聖安東尼奧，幫忙照顧他的小孩時，她也禮貌地拒絕了。在友好的討論一年後，她終於同意。今日，他們家三代人都認為這次搬家非常成功，因為這給予他們比起原先住在不同都市時，更親密的關係。

* Ms. 〔mɪz〕 *n.* …女士【不知某女性是未婚或已婚時使用】
  Garza 〔ˈgɑrzə〕 *n.* 加爾札【姓氏名】
  Brownsville 〔ˈbraʊnz͵vɪl〕 *n.* 布朗斯維爾【德克薩斯州（Texas
  〔ˈtɛksəs〕）最南部的都市】

move away 搬走；離開

San Antonio〔͵sæn ænˈtonɪo〕*n.* 聖安東尼奧【位於德州中南部，是德州第二大都市】

politely〔pəˈlaɪtlɪ〕*adv.* 有禮貌地

refuse〔rɪˈfjuz〕*v.* 拒絕　　friendly〔ˈfrɛndlɪ〕*adj.* 友好的

discussion〔dɪˈskʌʃən〕*n.* 討論；商議

generation〔͵dʒɛnəˈreʃən〕*n.* 世代

regard *A* ***as*** *B* 視 A 為 B；認為 A 是 B

success〔səkˈsɛs〕*n.* 成功

close〔klos〕*adj.* 接近的；親密的

relationship〔rɪˈleʃən͵ʃɪp〕*n.* 關係；親屬關係

separate〔ˈsɛpərɪt〕*adj.* 分開的；不同的

1. (**A**) Why was Garza's move a success?

   為什麼加爾札搬家成功？

   (A) It strengthened her family ties.

   　　這強化了她的家庭關係。

   (B) It improved her living conditions.

   　　這改善了她的生活狀況。

   * strengthen〔ˈstrɛŋθən〕*v.* 增加；加強

   　 ties〔taɪz〕*n. pl.* 關係

   　 improve〔ɪmˈpruv〕*v.* 改善

   　 condition〔kənˈdɪʃən〕*n.* 狀況

TEST 64

【2016 高考全國卷】

When Sandra Day O'Connor finished third in her class at Stanford Law School in 1952, she could not find work at a law firm because she was a woman. She became an Arizona state senator and, in 1981, the first woman to join the U.S. Supreme Court. O'Connor gave the deciding vote in many important cases during her 24 years on the top court.

1. What was the reason for O'Connor's being rejected by law firms?

    A. Her lack of proper training in law.

    B. The discrimination against women.

TEST 65

【2016 高考天津卷】

When John was growing up, other kids felt sorry for him. His parents always had him weeding the garden, carrying out the garbage and delivering newspapers. But when John reached adulthood, he was better off than his childhood playmates. He had more job satisfaction and a better marriage and was healthier. Most of all, he was happier. Far happier.

1. What do we know about John?

   A. He enjoyed his career and marriage.

   B. He was envied by others in his childhood.

TEST 64 詳解

【2016 高考全國卷】

When Sandra Day O'Connor finished third in her class at Stanford Law School in 1952, she could not find work *at a law firm because* she was a woman. She became an Arizona state senator *and*, *in 1981*, the first woman *to join the U.S. Supreme Court*. O'Connor gave the deciding vote *in many important cases during her 24 years on the top court*.

　　在 1952 年，當珊卓拉・戴・歐康納以全班第三名畢業於史丹佛大學法學院時，她在法律事務所找不到工作，因爲她是女性。她成爲亞歷桑那州的參議員，1981 年成爲第一位加入美國最高法院的女性。她在最高法院 24 年以來，歐康納在許多重要案件中，都投下了決定性的一票。

* Sandra Day O'Connor〔ˈsændrə ˌde oˈkɑnɚ〕*n.*
珊卓拉・戴・歐康納【1930-，美國法學家，她是美國最高法院首位女大法官，於 2006 年退休】
Stanford University〔ˈstænfɚd〕*n.* 史丹佛大學【位於美國加州的私立大學，鄰近汐谷，是全世界最知名的高等學府之一】
law〔lɔ〕*n.* 法律　　*law school* 法學院
firm〔fɝm〕*n.* 公司　　*law firm* 法律事務所
Arizona〔ˌærəˈzonə〕*n.* 亞利桑那州【位於美國西南部一州，首府鳳凰城（Phoenix〔ˈfinɪks〕）】

state〔stet〕*n., adj.* 州（的）　　senator〔'sɛnətɚ〕*n.* 參議員

supreme〔sə'prim〕*adj.* 最高的

court〔kort〕*n.* 法庭；法院

decide〔dɪ'saɪd〕*v.* 決定　　vote〔vot〕*n.* 投票

case〔kes〕*n.* 案件　　top〔tɑp〕*adj.* 最高的

1. (**B**) What was the reason for O'Connor's being rejected by law firms?　歐康納被法律事務所拒絕的原因是什麼？

   (A) Her lack of proper training in law.
      她缺乏法律的適當訓練。

   (B) The discrimination against women. <u>對女性的歧視。</u>

   * reject〔rɪ'dʒɛkt〕*v.* 拒絕　　lack〔læk〕*n.* 缺乏；缺少
     proper〔'prɑpɚ〕*adj.* 適當的
     training〔'trenɪŋ〕*n.* 訓練
     discrimination〔dɪˌskrɪmə'neʃən〕*n.* 歧視；差別待遇
     against〔ə'gɛnst〕*prep.* 反對；對抗

TEST 65 詳解

【 2016 高考天津卷 】

***When** John was growing up*, other kids felt sorry for him.

His parents *always* had him weeding the garden, carrying out

the garbage *and* delivering newspapers. ***But when** John*

reached adulthood, he was better off *than his childhood*

playmates. He had more job satisfaction and a better marriage

and was healthier. *Most of all*, he was happier. *Far* happier.

當約翰逐漸長大時，其他小孩都為他感到難過。他的父母總是叫他去花園除草、拿垃圾出去丟，還有送報紙。但是當約翰成年時，他比他的童年玩伴們都富有。他的工作滿意度更好、婚姻更幸福，而且身體更健康。最重要的是，他更快樂。快樂很多。

* kid〔kɪd〕*n.* 小孩　　weed〔wid〕*v.* 除草
  garbage〔'gɑrbɪdʒ〕*n.* 垃圾；廢物
  deliver〔dɪ'lɪvɚ〕*v.* 遞送　　reach〔ritʃ〕*v.* 達到；及
  adulthood〔ə'dʌlthʊd〕*n.* 成年時期
  be better off 更富有【是 be well off（富有）的比較級】
  childhood〔'tʃaɪld,hʊd〕*n.* 童年時期
  playmate〔'ple,met〕*n.* 玩伴
  satisfaction〔,sætɪs'fækʃən〕*n.* 滿足；滿意
  marriage〔'mærɪdʒ〕*n.* 婚姻　　healthy〔'hɛlθɪ〕*adj.* 健康的
  most of all 最重要的是（= *most important of all*）
  far〔fɑr〕*adv.* 遠地；大大地【修飾比較級】

1. (**A**) What do we know about John?
   關於約翰我們知道什麼？
   (A) He enjoyed his career and marriage.
   　　他享受他的事業和婚姻。
   (B) He was envied by others in his childhood.
   　　在童年時他被其他人羨慕。

   * enjoy〔ɪn'dʒɔɪ〕*v.* 享受　　career〔kə'rɪr〕*n.* 事業
     envy〔'ɛnvɪ〕*v.* 羨慕；嫉妒

TEST 66

【2016 高考全國卷】

Nurses and other care-givers need to be aware of the possible meanings of silence so that a patient's silence is not interrupted too early or allowed to go on unnecessarily. A nurse who understands the healing value of silence can use this understanding to assist in the care of patients.

1. What does the author advise nurses to do about silence?

   A. Break it while treating patients.

   B. Make use of its healing effects.

TEST　67

【 2016 高考浙江卷 】

A scientist working in his lab and a six-month-old baby playing with his food might seem to have little in common. After all, the scientist is engaged in serious research to uncover the nature of the physical world, and the baby is just playing, right? Perhaps, but some developmental psychologists have argued that this "play" is more like a scientific investigation than one might think.

1. According to some developmental psychologists, _____.

   A. a baby's play is nothing more than a game

   B. a baby's play is somehow similar to a scientist's experiment

TEST 66 詳解

【2016 高考全國卷】

Nurses and other care-givers need to be aware of the possible meanings *of silence **so that** a patient's silence is not interrupted too early **or** allowed to go on unnecessarily.* A nurse *who understands the healing value of silence* can use this understanding *to assist in the care of patients.*

護士和其他照顧者必須要知道沈默可能的意義，才不會太早打斷病人的沈默，或是讓沈默不必要地持續下去。了解沈默的療效的護士，可以利用這個理解來協助照顧病人。

* care-giver〔ˈkɛrˌɡɪvɚ〕*n.* 照顧者
  aware〔əˈwɛr〕*adj.* 注意到的；察覺的 <*of*>
  meaning〔ˈminɪŋ〕*n.* 意思；意義
  silence〔ˈsaɪləns〕*n.* 沈默
  so that 為了；以便　　patient〔ˈpeʃənt〕*n.* 病人
  interrupt〔ˌɪntəˈrʌpt〕*v.* 打斷；中斷
  allow〔əˈlaʊ〕*v.* 允許　　***go on*** 繼續
  unnecessarily〔ʌnˈnɛsəˌsɛrəlɪ〕*adv.* 不必要地
  healing〔ˈhilɪŋ〕*adj.* 治療的
  value〔ˈvælju〕*n.* 價值　　***healing value*** 療效
  assist〔əˈsɪst〕*v.* 幫助　　care〔kɛr〕*n.* 照顧

1. (**B**) What does the author advise nurses to do about silence?

關於沈默，作者建議護士們做什麼？

(A) Break it while treating patients.

治療病人時打破沈默。

(B) Make use of its healing effects.

利用沈默的治療效果。

* author〔ˈɔθɚ〕*n.* 作者　　advise〔ədˈvaɪz〕*v.* 忠告；建議

treat〔trit〕*v.* 治療　　***make use of*** 利用

effect〔əˈfɛkt〕*n.* 結果；影響；效果

TEST 67 詳解

【**2016 高考浙江卷**】

A scientist *working in his lab* **and** a six-month-old baby

playing with his food might seem to have little in common.

After all, the scientist is engaged in serious research *to*

uncover the nature of the physical world, **and** the baby is

just playing, right? Perhaps, **but** some developmental

psychologists have argued **that** this "*play*" is more like a

scientific investigation **than** one might think.

　　在實驗室工作的科學家，和在玩食物的六個月大小嬰兒，可能好像沒有什麼共同點。畢竟，科學家是在從事認眞的研究，以發掘自然界的本質，而小嬰兒只是在玩，是嗎？或許吧，但是有些發展心理學家主張，這種「玩樂」比一個人可能認爲的，更像是科學調查。

* lab〔læb〕*n.* 實驗室　　common〔'kamən〕*adj.* 常見的
have little in common 共同點很少
after all 畢竟　　***be engaged in*** 從事；參與
serious〔'sɪrɪəs〕*adj.* 嚴肅的；認眞的
research〔'risɜtʃ, rɪ'sɜtʃ〕*n.* 研究
uncover〔ʌn'kʌvə〕*v.* 揭露；揭發　　nature〔'netʃə〕*n.* 本質
physical〔'fɪzɪkl̩〕*adj.* 身體的；自然（界）的
perhaps〔pə'hæps〕*adv.* 或許；可能
developmental〔dɪ,vɛləp'mɛntl̩〕*adj.* 發展的
psychologist〔saɪ'kalədʒɪst〕*n.* 心理學家
argue〔'argju〕*v.* 主張　　scientific〔,saɪən'tɪfɪk〕*adj.* 科學的
investigation〔ɪn,vɛstə'geʃən〕*n.* 調查；研究

1. (**B**) According to some developmental psychologists,

　　_____.

　　根據一些發展心理學家的說法，_____。

(A) a baby's play is nothing more than a game
　　嬰兒玩樂只不過是玩遊戲而已

(B) a baby's play is somehow similar to a scientist's
　　experiment 嬰兒玩樂某些方面類似科學家做實驗

* ***nothing more than*** 只不過是
somehow〔'sʌm,haʊ〕*adv.* 設法；以某種方法
similar〔'sɪmələ〕*adj.* 類似的；相似的 < *to* >
experiment〔ɪk'spɛrəmənt〕*n.* 實驗

TEST　68

【2016 高考天津卷】

There is one very exhausting experience called "start-up fatigue". People with this tiredness will keep putting off a task because it is either too boring or too difficult. And the longer they delay it, the more tired they feel. Such fatigue is very real, even if not actually physical. The solution is obvious though not easy to apply: always handle the most difficult job first.

1. What does the author recommend doing to prevent start-up fatigue?

　A. Leaving out the toughest ideas.

　B. Dealing with the hardest task first.

TEST 68 詳解

【2016 高考天津卷】

There is one very exhausting experience *called "start-up fatigue"*. People *with this tiredness* will keep putting off a task *because* it is *either* too boring *or* too difficult. *And the longer they delay it, **the** more tired* they feel. Such fatigue is very real, *even **if** not actually physical*. The solution is obvious ***though** not easy to apply: always* handle the most difficult job *first*.

有一種非常令人疲倦的經驗，稱作「初始疲倦」。有這種疲倦感的人會一直拖延一件工作，因爲工作不是太無聊，就是太困難。而且工作拖得越久，他們就越感到疲倦。這樣的疲倦即使不是眞正身體上的，也非常眞實。解決方法很明顯，不過不容易做到：總是要先處理最困難的工作。

> * exhausting〔ɪgˈzɔstɪŋ〕*adj.* 令人疲倦的
> start-up〔ˈstɑrt͵ʌp〕*n.* 開始；起動
> fatigue〔fəˈtig〕*n.* 疲倦；疲勞
> tiredness〔ˈtaɪrdnɪs〕*n.* 疲倦；疲乏
> ***put off*** 拖延；延誤（= delay）

task〔tæsk〕*n.* 任務；工作

***either** A **or** B* 不是 A 就是 B

boring〔'bɔrɪŋ〕*adj.* 令人厭煩的；無聊的

delay〔dɪ'le〕*v.* 拖延；延誤

actually〔'æktʃʊəlɪ〕*adv.* 實際上；實際地

physical〔'fɪzɪkl̩〕*adj.* 身體上的

solution〔sə'luʃən〕*n.* 解決方法；解答

obvious〔'ɑbvɪəs〕*adj.* 明顯的

apply〔ə'plaɪ〕*v.* 應用；專心致力

handle〔'hændl̩〕*v.* 處理；應付

1. (**B**) What does the author recommend doing to prevent
start-up fatigue?

   作者建議做什麼來防止初始疲倦？

   (A) Leaving out the toughest ideas.

   　　忽略最困難的構想。

   (B) Dealing with the hardest task first.

   　　<u>先處理最困難的工作。</u>

   * author〔'ɔθɚ〕*n.* 作者

   　recommend〔ˌrɛkə'mɛnd〕*v.* 勸告；建議

   　prevent〔prɪ'vɛnt〕*v.* 防止；預防

   　leave out 忽略；遺漏　　tough〔tʌf〕*adj.* 困難的

   　idea〔aɪ'diə〕*n.* 主意；構想

   　deal with 處理；應付（ = *handle* ）

TEST 69

【2016 高考天津卷】

Every man wants his son to be somewhat of a clone, not in features but in footsteps. As he grows you also age, and your ambitions become more unachievable. You begin to realize that your boy, in your footsteps, could probably accomplish what you hoped for.

1. What was the author's hope for his son?
   A. To resemble him in appearance.
   B. To reach the author's unachievable goals.

TEST 70

【2016 高考四川卷】

In the depth of the French Guianese rainforest, there still remain some indigenous people. People in this area are in fact French citizens because it is a French territory. In theory, they should live by the French law. However, their remote locations mean that the French law is often ignored or unknown. They live largely by their own laws and social customs.

1. What does the author say about the indigenous people in French Guiana?

   A. They seldom follow the French law.

   B. They often ignore the Guianese law.

TEST 69 詳解

【2016 高考天津卷】

Every man wants his son to be somewhat of a clone, *not in features but in footsteps.* *As he grows* you *also* age, *and* your ambitions become more unachievable. You begin to realize *that* your boy, *in your footsteps, could probably accomplish what you hoped for.*

——受詞——

　　每一個男人都想要他的兒子多少是自己的翻版,不是五官上,而是自己的腳步。隨著他長大,你也會變老,而你的抱負也變得更加無法達到了。你開始了解到,你的兒子,跟隨著你的腳步,可能可以達成你所希望的。

* somewhat〔'sʌm,hwɑt〕*pron.* 多少;有點
  somewhat of 多少;有幾分　　clone〔klon〕*n.* 複製品;翻版
  feature〔'fitʃɚ〕*n.* 特徵;特色;(pl.) 五官
  footstep〔'fut,stɛp〕*n.* 腳步;步伐【此指 follow in sb.'s
  footsteps 跟隨某人的腳步】
  age〔edʒ〕*v.* 變老　　ambition〔æm'bɪʃən〕*n.* 雄心;抱負
  unachievable〔,ʌnə'tʃivəbḷ〕*adj.* 無法完成的;無法達到的
  realize〔'rɪə,laɪz〕*v.* 了解;理解
  probably〔'prɑbəblɪ〕*adv.* 可能
  accomplish〔ə'kʌmplɪʃ〕*v.* 達成;完成

1.(**B**)　What was the author's hope for his son?

作者對他的兒子有什麼希望？

(A) To resemble him in appearance. 外表長得像他。

(B) To reach the author's unachievable goals.

達成作者無法完成的目標。

* author〔ˋɔθɚ〕*n.* 作者

　resemble〔rɪˋzɛmbḷ〕*v.* 相像

　appearance〔əˋpɪrəns〕*n.* 外表

　reach〔ritʃ〕*v.* 到達；達成　　goal〔gol〕*n.* 目標

TEST　70　詳解

【2016 高考四川卷】

In the depth of the French Guianese rainforest, there *still*

remain some indigenous people.　People *in this area* are *in*

fact French citizens ***because*** *it is a French territory.　In*

theory, they should live *by the French law.　However*, their

remote locations mean ***that*** *the French law is often ignored*

or unknown.　They live *largely by their own laws* ***and*** *social*

customs.

在法屬圭亞納的雨林深處，還遺留著一些原住民。這個地區的人事實上是法國公民，因爲這裡是法國的領土。理論上，他們應該遵照法國的法律生活。然而，他們這麼遙遠的位置意味著，法國的法律通常被忽略或不爲人知。他們主要是按照自己的法律和社會習俗來生活。

* depth〔dɛpθ〕*n.* 深度；深處
  French Guianese〔frɛntʃ ˏgɪæn'iz〕*adj.* 法屬圭亞納的
  【French Guiana〔frɛntʃ gɪ'ænə〕*n.* 法屬圭亞納，位於南美洲】
  rainforest〔'renˏfɔrɪst〕*n.* 雨林
  remain〔rɪ'men〕*v.* 剩下；遺留
  indigenous〔ɪn'dɪdʒənəs〕*adj.* 原產的；固有的
  area〔'ɛrɪə〕*n.* 地區　　citizen〔'sɪtəzn〕*n.* 公民
  territory〔'tɛrəˏtorɪ〕*n.* 領土　　theory〔'θiərɪ〕*n.* 理論
  in theory 理論上　　by〔baɪ〕*prep.* 根據；按照
  remote〔rɪ'mot〕*adj.* 偏僻的；遙遠的
  location〔lo'keʃən〕*n.* 位置；地方
  mean〔min〕*v.* 意謂；表示　　ignore〔ɪg'nor〕*v.* 忽視
  unknown〔ʌn'non〕*adj.* 未知的；不爲人知的
  largely〔'lɑrdʒlɪ〕*adv.* 主要地　　social〔'soʃəl〕*adj.* 社會的
  custom〔'kʌstəm〕*n.* 風俗；習慣

1. (**A**) What does the author say about the indigenous people in French Guiana?

   有關法屬圭亞納的原住民作者說了什麼？

   (A) They seldom follow the French law.

   　　他們很少遵循法國的法律。

   (B) They often ignore the Guianese law.

   　　他們時常忽視圭亞納的法律。

   * author〔'ɔθɚ〕*n.* 作者　　seldom〔'sɛldəm〕*adv.* 很少
     follow〔'fɑlo〕*v.* 遵循

TEST 71

【2016 高考四川卷】

Researchers have discovered that those given milk taken from cows at night, which contains 10 times the amount of melatonin, were less active and less anxious than those fed with the milk collected during daytime. While the effect of cow milk harvested at different times has not been tested on humans up to now, taking melatonin drugs has been suggested to those who are struggling to fall asleep at night.

1. Which of the following is true of melatonin according to the text?

   A. It can make people more energetic.

   B. It's used in sleeping drugs.

TEST 71 詳解

【2016 高考四川卷】

Researchers have discovered ***that*** *those* *given milk taken*

from cows at night, ***which*** *contains 10 times the amount of*

melatonin, *were less active* ***and*** *less anxious* ***than*** *those fed*

with the milk collected during daytime. ***While*** *the effect* *of*

cow milk harvested at different times *has not been tested on*

humans up to now, taking melatonin drugs has been suggested

to those ***who*** *are struggling to fall asleep at night.*

　　研究人員已經發現，被餵食夜晚收集的牛奶的人，夜奶含有十倍褪黑激素，比起被餵食白天收集的牛奶的人，比較不活躍、比較不焦慮。雖然在不同時間收集的乳牛牛奶的影響，到目前為止還沒有在人類身上做測試，那些晚上努力想睡著的人，已經有人建議服用褪黑激素的藥物。

　　* researcher〔rɪˈsɝtʃɚ〕*n.* 研究人員
　　discover〔dɪˈskʌvɚ〕*v.* 發現
　　cow〔kau〕*n.* 母牛；乳牛

contain〔kən'ten〕v. 包含；包括

time〔taɪm〕n. 倍數；時間

amount〔ə'maʊnt〕n. 數量

melatonin〔,mɛlə'tonɪn〕n. 褪黑激素

less〔lɛs〕adv. 比較不…

active〔'æktɪv〕adj. 活躍的；活潑的

anxious〔'æŋkʃəs〕adj. 憂慮的；擔心的

feed〔fid〕v. 餵食　　collect〔kə'lɛkt〕v. 收集

during〔'dʊrɪŋ〕prep. 在…期間

daytime〔'de,taɪm〕n. 白天

effect〔ɪ'fɛkt〕n. 效果；影響

harvest〔'hɑrvɪst〕v. 收穫；收成

test〔tɛst〕v. 測試　　human〔'hjumən〕n. 人類；人

up to now 直到現在　　drug〔drʌg〕n. 藥

suggest〔sə(g)'dʒɛst〕v. 提議；建議

struggle〔'strʌgl〕v. 掙扎；努力　　***fall asleep*** 睡著

1. (**B**) Which of the following is true of melatonin according to the text?

根據本文，下列何者適用於褪黑激素？

(A) It can make people more energetic.

它可以使人更加精力充沛。

(B) It's used in sleeping drugs.

<u>它被用在安眠藥中。</u>

* following〔'fɑloɪŋ〕adj. 下列的；以下的

be true of 適用於　　text〔tɛkst〕n. 本文

energetic〔,ɛnɚ'dʒɛtɪk〕adj. 精力充沛的

sleeping drug 安眠藥

TEST 72

【2016 高考浙江卷】

Look at the baby playing. Babies are not born knowing basic facts of the universe. They form an understanding through repeated experiments and then build on the knowledge to learn more. Though their ranges and tools differ, the baby's investigation and the scientist's experiment appear to share the same aim (to learn about the natural world) and overall approach (gathering direct evidence from the world).

1. We learn from the paragraph that _____.

    A. scientists and babies seem to observe the world differently

    B. babies seem to collect evidence just as scientists do

TEST 72 詳解

【2016 高考浙江卷】

Look at the baby playing. Babies are not born *knowing basic facts of the universe.* They form an understanding *through repeated experiments **and** then* build on the knowledge to learn more. ***Though*** *their ranges and tools differ,* the baby's investigation **and** the scientist's experiment appear to
　　　　　　　　主　詞　　　　　　　　　　　　　　 V.
share the same aim (*to learn about the natural world*) ***and*** overall approach (*gathering direct evidence from the world*).

　　看看嬰兒玩的樣子。嬰兒並不是出生就知道宇宙的基本事實。他們是透過不斷的實驗形成理解，然後再基於這些知識學習更多。雖然範圍和工具不同，但嬰兒的調查和科學家的實驗，似乎有相同的目標（學習有關自然界的事物），和整體的方法（從這個世界收集直接的證據）。

* basic〔`besɪk〕*adj.* 基本的
  universe〔`junə͵vɝs〕*n.* 宇宙；世界
  form〔fɔrm〕*v.* 形成；產生
  understanding〔͵ʌndɚ`stændɪŋ〕*n.* 理解
  through〔θru〕*prep.* 通過；透過

repeated〔rɪ'pitɪd〕*adj.* 重複的；不斷的

experiment〔ɪk'spɛrəmənt〕*n.* 實驗

build on 依賴；以～爲基礎

knowledge〔'nɑlɪdʒ〕*n.* 知識

range〔rendʒ〕*n.* 範圍　　tool〔tul〕*n.* 工具

differ〔'dɪfɚ〕*v.* 不同；有差異

investigation〔ɪn͵vɛstə'geʃən〕*n.* 調查

scientist〔'saɪəntɪst〕*n.* 科學家

appear〔ə'pɪr〕*v.* 似乎；好像　　share〔ʃɛr〕*v.* 共享；分享

aim〔em〕*n.* 目標　　natural〔'nætʃərəl〕*adj.* 自然的

overall〔'ovɚ͵ɔl〕*adj.* 整體的；全面的

approach〔ə'protʃ〕*n.* 方法

gather〔'gæðɚ〕*v.* 聚集；收集

direct〔də'rɛkt〕*adj.* 直接的

evidence〔'ɛvədəns〕*n.* 證據

1. (**B**) We learn from the paragraph that _____.

　　從本段我們得知，_____。

　　(A) scientists and babies seem to observe the world
　　　　differently
　　　　科學家和嬰兒觀察世界的方法似乎不同

　　(B) babies seem to collect evidence just as scientists do
　　　　嬰兒似乎在收集證據，就像科學家一樣

　　* learn〔lɜn〕*v.* 得知　　observe〔əb'zɜv〕*v.* 觀察
　　　differently〔'dɪfərəntlɪ〕*adv.* 不同地；有差別地
　　　collect〔kə'lɛkt〕*v.* 收集

TEST 73

【2016 高考浙江卷】

An important negative effect of gossip is that it can hurt the person being talked about. Usually, gossip spreads information that a person would rather keep secret. The more embarrassing or shameful the secret is, the juicier the gossip it makes. Probably the worse type of gossip is the absolute lie. People often think of gossip as harmless, but cruel lies can cause pain.

1. An important negative effect of gossip is that it _____.

　A. spreads information around

　B. causes unpleasant experiences

TEST 73 詳解

【2016 高考浙江卷】

An important negative effect *of gossip* is ***that*** *it can hurt*

the person being talked about. *Usually*, gossip spreads

information ***that*** *a person would rather keep secret.* *The more*

embarrassing or shameful the secret is, ***the*** juicier the gossip

it makes. *Probably* the worse type *of gossip* is the absolute

lie. People *often* think of gossip as harmless, ***but*** cruel lies

can cause pain.

　　八卦有一個重要的負面影響，就是它可能會傷害到被談論的那個
人。通常，八卦就是散播一個人寧可保密的消息。這個秘密越難堪或越
丟臉，這個八卦就越精彩。也許最糟糕的一種八卦是完全的謊言。人們
經常認為八卦是無害的，但殘酷的謊言可能會導致痛苦。

> * negative (ˈnɛgətɪv) *adj.* 否定的；負面的
> effect (ɪˈfɛkt) *n.* 影響
> gossip (ˈgɑsəp) *n.* 閒話；八卦
> hurt (hɜt) *v.* 傷害　　***talk about*** 談論
> spread (sprɛd) *v.* 流傳；傳播
> information (ˌɪnfəˈmeʃən) *n.* 消息；報導

would rather V 寧願

secret〔'sikrɪt〕*adj.* 祕密的　*n.* 祕密

embarrassing〔ɪm'bærəsɪŋ〕*adj.* 令人尷尬的；令人難堪的

shameful〔'ʃemfəl〕*adj.* 可恥的；丟臉的

juicy〔'dʒusɪ〕*adj.* 多汁的；有趣的；生動的

probably〔'prabəblɪ〕*adv.* 可能地

type〔taɪp〕*n.* 種類

absolute〔'æbsəˌlut〕*adj.* 絕對的；完全的

harmless〔'harmlɪs〕*adj.* 無害的；無惡意的

think of A as B 視 A 為 B；認為 A 是 B

cruel〔'kruəl〕*adj.* 冷酷的；殘酷的

pain〔pen〕*n.* 痛苦

1. (**B**) An important negative effect of gossip is that it

    _____.

    八卦有一個重要的負面影響是，它會 _____ 。

    (A) spreads information around
       四處傳播消息

    (B) causes unpleasant experiences
       造成令人不愉快的經驗

    * around〔ə'raʊnd〕*adv.* 四處；到處
      unpleasant〔ʌn'plɛznt〕*adj.* 令人不愉快的

TEST 74

【2016 高考北京卷】

For previous generations, college was a decisive break from parental control. In the past two decades, however, continued connection with and dependence on family, thanks to cell phones, email and social media, have increased significantly. Some parents go so far as to help with coursework. College is no longer seen as a <u>passage</u> from the shelter of the family to autonomy and adult responsibility.

1. What does the underlined word "<u>passage</u>" in the paragraph mean?

   A. change

   B. choice

TEST 74 詳解

【2016 高考北京卷】

For previous generations, college was a decisive break *from parental control. In the past two decades, however,* continued connection with and dependence on family,
主　詞

thanks to cell phones, email and social media, have increased
V.

significantly. Some parents go *so far* as to help with *coursework.* College is *no longer* seen as a passage *from the shelter of the family to autonomy and adult responsibility.*

　　對以前的世代而言，上大學是脫離父母控制決定性的時候。然而，在過去二十年來，因爲有了手機、電子郵件和社群媒體，與家人的連結以及對家人的依賴都大大地增加。有些家長甚至幫忙做課程作業。大學已經不再被認爲是從家庭庇護到自主和成年責任的變遷。

> * previous〔ˈprivɪəs〕*adj.* 之前的；以前的
> generation〔ˌdʒɛnəˈreʃən〕*n.* 世代
> college〔ˈkɑlɪdʒ〕*n.* 大學；學院
> decisive〔dɪˈsaɪsɪv〕*adj.* 決定性的；重大的

break〔brek〕*n.* 轉變；中斷

parental〔pə'rɛntḷ〕*adj.* 父母親的

past〔pæst〕*adj.* 過去的　　decade〔'dɛked〕*n.* 十年

continued〔kən'tɪnjud〕*adj.* 持續的

connection〔kə'nɛkʃən〕*n.* 連結；關聯＜*with*＞

dependence〔dɪ'pɛndəns〕*n.* 依賴＜*on*＞

thanks to 因為；由於　　***cell phone*** 行動電話；手機

email〔'i,mel〕*n.* 電子郵件

social〔'soʃəl〕*adj.* 社會的；社交的

media〔'midɪə〕*n.* 媒體　　***social media*** 社群媒體

increase〔ɪn'kris〕*v.* 增加；提高

significantly〔sɪg'nɪfəkəntlɪ〕*adv.* 相當大地；顯著地

go so far as to V 甚至做…

coursework〔'kors,wɝk〕*n.* 課程作業

no longer 不再　　***be seen as*** 被認為是

passage〔'pæsɪdʒ〕*n.* 遷移；變遷

shelter〔'ʃɛltɚ〕*n.* 庇護所；避難所

autonomy〔ɔ'tɑnəmɪ〕*n.* 自治；自主性

adult〔ə'dʌlt〕*adj.* 成人的

responsibility〔rɪ,spɑnsə'bɪlətɪ〕*n.* 責任；義務

1.（**A**）What does the underlined word "<u>passage</u>" in the

　　　paragraph mean?

　　　本段中畫底線的 passage 是什麼意思？

　　　(A) change 改變

　　　(B) choice 選擇

　　　* underline〔,ʌndɚ'laɪn〕*v.* 畫底線

　　　　paragraph〔'pærə,græf〕*n.* 段落　　mean〔min〕*v.* 意思是

　　　　change〔tʃendʒ〕*n.* 改變　　choice〔tʃɔɪs〕*n.* 選擇

TEST 75

【2016 高考江蘇卷】

Chimps in the wild seek food for themselves. Even chimp mothers regularly decline to share food with their children, who are able from a young age to gather their own food. Chimps have little instinct to help one another. In the laboratory, chimps don't share food either. If they are in a cage, they don't care whether their neighbor gets fed or not. Chimps are truly selfish.

1. What can we learn from the experiment with chimps?

   A. Chimps seldom care about others' interests.

   B. Chimps tend to provide food for their children.

TEST 75 詳解

【2016 高考江蘇卷】

Chimps *in the wild* seek food *for themselves.* *Even*

chimp mothers *regularly* decline to share food *with their*

children, who *are able from a young age to gather their own*

food. Chimps have little instinct to help one another. *In the*

laboratory, chimps don't share food *either.* ***If they are in a***

cage, they don't care whether *their neighbor gets fed or not.*
名詞子句做受詞

Chimps are *truly* selfish.

　　野生的黑猩猩會自己覓食。即使是黑猩猩媽媽，也經常拒絕和小孩分享食物，黑猩猩小孩從很小就能夠自己找食物了。黑猩猩沒有什麼互相幫助的本能。在實驗室裡，黑猩猩也不會分享食物。如果在籠子裡，牠們不會在意牠們的鄰居是否被餵食。黑猩猩真的很自私。

　　* chimp〔tʃɪmp〕*n.* 黑猩猩【源自 chimpanzee〔ˌtʃɪmpænˈzi〕】
　　 wild〔waɪld〕*n.* 荒野；野地；野生狀態
　　 seek〔sik〕*v.* 尋求　　*for* oneself 自己
　　 regularly〔ˈrɛgjələlɪ〕*adv.* 經常地
　　 decline〔dɪˈklaɪn〕*v.* 拒絕　　share〔ʃɛr〕*v.* 分享

be able to V 能夠　　age〔edʒ〕*n.* 年紀

gather〔'gæðə〕*v.* 聚集；收集

instinct〔'ɪnstɪŋkt〕*n.* 本能

one another 彼此；互相

laboratory〔'læbərə,torɪ〕*n.* 實驗室（= *lab*）

either〔'iðə〕*adv.* 也（不）【用於否定句】

cage〔kedʒ〕*n.* 籠子

whether〔'hwɛðə〕*conj.* 是否【可與 or not 連用】

neighbor〔'nebə〕*n.* 鄰居　　feed〔fid〕*v.* 餵食

truly〔'trulɪ〕*adv.* 真正地　　selfish〔'sɛlfɪʃ〕*adj.* 自私的

1.（ **A** ）What can we learn from the experiment with chimps?

　　從這個黑猩猩的實驗我們得知什麼？

　　(A) Chimps seldom care about others' interests.

　　　　<u>黑猩猩很少關心他人的利益。</u>

　　(B) Chimps tend to provide food for their children.

　　　　黑猩猩通常會提供食物給牠們的小孩。

　　* learn〔lɜn〕*v.* 得知

　　　experiment〔ɪk'spɛrəmənt〕*n.* 實驗

　　　seldom〔'sɛldəm〕*adv.* 很少

　　　interest〔'ɪntrɪst〕*n.* 興趣；利益

　　　tend to V 傾向於；通常

　　　provide〔prə'vaɪd〕*v.* 提供

TEST 76

【2016 高考江蘇卷】

The most recent powerful El Niños caused tremendous damage around the globe. But such El Niños come with months of warning, and governments CAN prepare. According to the Overseas Development Institute (ODI), however, just 12% of disaster-relief funding has gone to reducing risks in advance, despite evidence that a dollar spent on risk-reduction saves at least two on reconstruction.

1. The data provided by ODI in the paragraph suggest that
   A. more investment should go to risk reduction.
   B. recovery and reconstruction should come first.

TEST 76 詳解

【2016 高考江蘇卷】

The most recent powerful El Niños caused tremendous

damage *around the globe.* ***But*** such El Niños come *with*

months of warning, ***and*** governments CAN prepare.

According to the Overseas Development Institute (ODI),

however, just 12% of disaster-relief funding has gone to

reducing risks *in advance, despite evidence* *that* a dollar

spent on risk-reduction saves at least two (dollars) on
　　　　　　that 子句做 evidence 的同位語

reconstruction.

　　最近以來的強烈聖嬰現象，導致全球極大的損失。但是這樣的聖嬰現象有幾個月的預警時間，政府是可以準備的。然而，根據「海外發展協會」（ODI）的資訊，救災基金中只有百分之 12，用於事先減少風險，但證據顯示，用於減少風險的一元，可以省下至少二元的重建。

* recent〔ˋrisn̩t〕*adj.* 最近的　　powerful〔ˋpauɚfəl〕*adj.* 強烈的
　El Niño〔ɛlˋninjo〕*n.* 聖嬰現象【指嚴重影響全球氣候的太平洋
　　熱帶海域的大風及海水的大規模移動】
　cause〔kɔz〕*v.* 導致　　tremendous〔trɪˋmɛndəs〕*adj.* 極大的

damage〔'dæmɪdʒ〕 n. 損害　　around〔ə'raʊnd〕 prep. 到處

globe〔glob〕 n. 球體；地球

around the globe 全球；全世界

warning〔'wɔrnɪŋ〕 n. 警告

government〔'gʌvənmənt〕 n. 政府

prepare〔prɪ'pɛr〕 v. 準備　　***according to*** 根據

overseas〔'ovə'siz〕 adj. 海外的

development〔dɪ'vɛləpmənt〕 n. 發展

institute〔'ɪnstə,tjut〕 n. 協會　　disaster〔dɪz'æstə〕 n. 災難

relief〔rɪ'lif〕 n. 減輕；救濟；救助

disaster-relief 災難救助　　funding〔'fʌndɪŋ〕 n. 基金

go to （錢、時間）被用在～　　reduce〔rɪ'djus〕 v. 減少

risk〔rɪsk〕 n. 危險；風險　　***in advance*** 事先

despite〔dɪ'spaɪt〕 prep. 儘管　　evidence〔'ɛvədəns〕 n. 證據

reduction〔rɪ'dʌkʃən〕 n. 減少

save〔sev〕 v. 節省　　***at least*** 至少

reconstruction〔,rikən'strʌkʃən〕 n. 重建

1. (**A**) The data provided by ODI in the paragraph suggest that
    段落中由 ODI 所提供的資料顯示，

    (A) more investment should go to risk reduction.
    <u>應該要有更多投資用於減少風險。</u>

    (B) recovery and reconstruction should come first.
    復原和重建應該優先。

    * data〔'detə〕 n. 資料　　provide〔prə'vaɪd〕 v. 提供
      suggest〔sə(g)'dʒɛst〕 v. 顯示；表示
      investment〔ɪn'vɛstmənt〕 n. 投資
      recovery〔rɪ'kʌvərɪ〕 n. 恢復；復原

TEST 77

【2016 高考江蘇卷】

Not long ago, most people didn't know Shelly-Ann Fraser-Pryce. However, Stephen Francis observed the eighteen-year-old girl and was convinced that he had seen the beginnings of true greatness. He sensed there was something trying to get out, something other coaches had overlooked. He decided to offer her strict training sessions. A few years later, at Jamaica's Olympic trials in early 2008, she beat the queen of the sprint.

1. Why did Stephen Francis decide to coach Shelly-Ann?

    A. He sensed a great potential in her.

    B. She suffered a lot of defeats at the previous track meets.

TEST 77 詳解

【2016 高考江蘇卷】

Not long ago, most people didn't know Shelly-Ann Fraser-Pryce. *However*, Stephen Francis observed the eighteen-year-old girl **and** was convinced **that** *he had seen the beginnings of true greatness*. He sensed there was something trying to get out, *something other coaches had overlooked*. He decided to offer her strict training sessions. *A few years later, at Jamaica's Olympic trials in early 2008,* she beat the queen *of the sprint*.

不久之前，大部分人還不認識謝莉-安・弗雷澤-普萊斯。然而，史蒂芬・法蘭西斯觀察到這個 18 歲的女孩，他確信他看到了真正偉大的開端。他感覺到有什麼東西想要破繭而出，其他教練都忽略的東西。他決定提供她嚴格的訓練課程。幾年之後，在 2008 年初牙買加的奧運預賽中，她打敗了短跑女王。

* Shelly-Ann Fraser-Pryce（ˈʃɛlɪˌæn ˈfrezɚˌpraɪs）
  n. 謝莉-安・弗雷澤-普萊斯【牙買加短跑運動員。
  2008 年奧運及 2012 年倫敦奧運女子 100 公尺冠軍】
  Stephen Francis（ˈstivən ˈfrænsɪs）*n.* 史蒂芬・法蘭西斯

observe〔əb'zɜv〕*v.* 觀察

convinced〔kən'vɪnst〕*adj.* 確信的

beginning〔bɪ'gɪnɪŋ〕*n.* 開始

greatness〔'gretnɪs〕*n.* 偉大　　sense〔sɛns〕*v.* 感覺（到）

get out 洩露；被人知道　　coach〔kotʃ〕*n.* 教練　*v.* 當教練

overlook〔͵ovɚ'luk〕*v.* 忽略　　decide〔dɪ'saɪd〕*v.* 決定

offer〔'ɔfɚ〕*v.* 提供　　strict〔strɪkt〕*adj.* 嚴格的

training〔'trenɪŋ〕*n.* 訓練　　session〔'sɛʃən〕*n.* 課程

Jamaica〔dʒə'mekə〕*n.* 牙買加【位於西印度群島】

Olympic〔o'lɪmpɪk〕*adj.* 奧運的

trial〔'traɪəl〕*n.* 試驗　　beat〔bit〕*v.* 擊敗

queen〔kwin〕*n.* 女王　　sprint〔sprɪnt〕*n.* 短跑

1. (**A**) Why did Stephen Francis decide to coach Shelly-Ann?

　　為什麼史蒂芬・法蘭西斯決定當謝莉-安的教練？

　　(A) He sensed a great potential in her despite.

　　　　<u>他感覺到她有很大的潛力。</u>

　　(B) She suffered a lot of defeats at the previous track
　　　　meets.

　　　　她在之前的徑賽大會遭受很多次失敗。

　　　* potential〔pə'tɛnʃəl〕*n.* 潛力

　　　　suffer〔'sʌfɚ〕*v.* 遭受　　defeat〔dɪ'fit〕*n.* 失敗

　　　　previous〔'privɪəs〕*adj.* 之前的

　　　　track〔træk〕*n.* 跑道；徑賽　　meet〔mit〕*n.* 運動會

TEST 78

【2016 高考四川卷】

Your personal lives are busy, but try to devote some of your time and energy to something much larger than yourself. Find an issue you are interested in and learn more. Volunteer or contribute a little money to a cause. Whatever you do, don't be a bystander. Get involved. You may have the opportunity to make a difference in the lives of others.

1. What does the author stress in the paragraph?
   A. Working hard to get a bigger opportunity.
   B. Rising above self and acting to help others.

TEST　79

【2015 高考全國卷】

When the chance came for a weekend in Florida, I excitedly left for the land of warmth and vitamin C, thinking of beaches and orange trees. Swimming pools, wine tasting, and pink sunsets filled the weekend, but the best part was a 7 a.m. adventure to a farmers' market that proved to be more than worth the early wake-up call.

1. What made the author's getting up early worthwhile?

   A. Walking in the morning sun.

   B. Visiting a local farmers' market.

TEST 78 詳解

【2016 高考四川卷】

Your personal lives are busy, ***but*** try to devote some of
your time and energy *to something much larger than yourself.*
Find an issue *you are interested in **and*** learn more. Volunteer
or contribute a little money *to a cause.* ***Whatever*** *you do,*
don't be a bystander. Get involved. You may have the
opportunity to make a difference *in the lives of others.*

　　你的個人生活很忙碌，但是請試著投入你的一些時間和精力，給某個大過於你自己的事情。找一個你感興趣的議題，多學習一點東西。去當義工，或是為了某個目標捐一點錢。無論你做什麼都好，就是不要做個旁觀者。要投入。你可能會有機會影響別人的生活。

* personal〔'pɝsn̩l〕*adj.* 個人的；私人的
  devote〔dɪ'vot〕*v.* 奉獻；投入
  energy〔'ɛnɚdʒɪ〕*n.* 精力；力量
  issue〔'ɪʃu〕*n.* 議題；問題　　***be interested in*** 對～感興趣
  volunteer〔,vɑlən'tɪr〕*v.* 自願；當義工
  contribute〔kən'trɪbjut〕*v.* 捐贈；捐助
  cause〔kɔs〕*n.* 理由；目標；理想
  whatever〔hwɑt'ɛvɚ〕*pron.* 不論什麼（= *no matter what*）

bystander〔'baɪˌstændɚ〕*n.* 旁觀者；局外人

involve〔ɪn'vɑlv〕*v.* 捲入；牽涉

opportunity〔ˌɑpɚ'tunətɪ〕*n.* 機會

make a difference 有差別；有影響

1. (**B**) What does the author stress in the paragraph?

在本段中作者強調什麼？

(A) Working hard to get a bigger opportunity.

努力工作以獲得更大的機會。

(B) Rising above self and acting to help others.

<u>超越自我並採取行動幫助他人。</u>

* author〔'ɔθɚ〕*n.* 作者　　stress〔strɛs〕*v.* 強調

paragraph〔'pærəˌgræf〕*n.* 段落

rise〔raɪz〕*v.* 升起；超越

above〔ə'bʌv〕*prep.* 在…之上；勝過

self〔sɛlf〕*n.* 自身；自己　　act〔ækt〕*v.* 採取行動

TEST 79 詳解

【 2015 高考全國卷 】

When *the chance came for a weekend in Florida*, I

excitedly left for the land *of warmth and vitamin C, thinking*

of beaches and orange trees. Swimming pools, wine tasting, and pink sunsets filled the weekend, ***but*** the best part was a

7 a.m. adventure *to a farmers' market **that** proved to be more*

than worth the early wake-up call.

　　當有機會到佛羅里達度週末時，我興奮地出發，前往這個充滿溫暖和維他命 C 的土地，心中想著海灘和柳橙樹。游泳池、品酒和粉紅色的夕陽充滿了整個週末，但是最棒的是早上七點鐘，到農夫市集的一場冒險，那證明了比一大早的叫醒電話更值得。

> * chance〔tʃæns〕 *n.* 機會
> Florida〔'flɔrədə〕 *n.* 佛羅里達州【位於美國東南部】
> excitedly〔ɪk'saɪtɪdlɪ〕 *adv.* 興奮地　　***leave for*** 出發前往
> land〔lænd〕 *n.* 土地　　warmth〔wɔrmθ〕 *n.* 溫暖
> vitamin〔'vaɪtəmɪn〕 *n.* 維他命　　taste〔test〕 *v.* 品嚐
> ***wine tasting*** 品酒　　pink〔pɪŋk〕 *adj.* 粉紅色的
> sunset〔'sʌn,sɛt〕 *n.* 日落　　fill〔fɪl〕 *v.* 充滿
> adventure〔əd'vɛntʃɚ〕 *n.* 冒險　　prove〔pruv〕 *v.* 證明
> worth〔wɝθ〕 *adj.* 值得的　　***wake-up call*** 電話叫醒服務

1. (**B**) What made the author's getting up early worthwhile?
　　什麼事情讓作者早起很值得？
　　(A) Walking in the morning sun.
　　　　在晨曦中散步。
　　(B) Visiting a local farmers' market.
　　　　<u>造訪當地的農夫市集。</u>

> * author〔'ɔθɚ〕 *n.* 作者
> worthwhile〔'wɝθ,hwaɪl〕 *adj.* 值得的
> local〔'lok!〕 *adj.* 當地的

TEST　80

【2015 高考全國卷】

Salvador Dali (1904-1989) was one of the most popular modern artists. There is now an exhibition of Dali, including over 200 paintings, sculptures, drawings and more. Among the works, you will find the best pieces, most importantly *The Persistence of Memory*. There is also *L'Enigme sans Fin* from 1938, projects for stage and screen and selected parts from television programs reflecting the artist's showman qualities.

1. What is Dali's *The Persistence of Memory* considered to be?

   A. One of his masterpieces.

   B. One of the best TV programs.

TEST 80 詳解

【2015 高考全國卷】

　　Salvador Dali (1904-1989) was one of the most popular modern artists.　There is now an exhibition *of Dali, including over 200 paintings, sculptures, drawings* **and** *more. Among the works,* you will find the best pieces, *most importantly The Persistence of Memory.*　There is *also L'Enigme sans Fin from 1938,* projects *for stage* **and** *screen* **and** selected parts *from television programs* reflecting the artist's showman qualities.

　　薩爾瓦多‧達利（1904-1989）是最受歡迎的現代藝術家之一。現在有一個達利的展覽，包括超過 200 件以上的油畫、雕刻、木炭畫等，其中你會看到最好的作品，最重要的是「記憶的堅持」（又譯為：記憶的永恆）。也有 1938 年的「無盡之謎」、搬上舞台或螢幕的計畫，還有來自電視節目的精選部分，都反映出這位藝術家愛表演的特質。

* Salvador Dali〔ˈsælvəˌdɔr ˈdɑlɪ〕 *n.* 薩爾瓦多‧達利
【1904-1989，西班牙畫家，以其超現實主義作品而聞名，他與畢卡索（Pablo Picasso）和米羅（Joan Miró），同被認為是西班牙 20 世紀最具代表性的三位畫家】
modern〔ˈmɑdən〕 *adj.* 現代的

artist〔ˋɑrtɪst〕 *n.* 藝術家　　exhibition〔͵ɛksəˋbɪʃən〕 *n.* 展覽

including〔 ɪnˋkludɪŋ 〕 *prep.* 包括

painting〔ˋpentɪŋ〕 *n.* 畫作【油畫、水彩畫等】

sculpture〔ˋskʌlptʃə〕 *n.* 雕刻（品）

drawing〔ˋdrɔɪŋ〕 *n.* 圖畫

　【鉛筆、木炭等描繪的】

work〔 wɜk 〕 *n.* 作品

piece〔 pis 〕 *n.* 作品

persistence〔 pəˋsɪstəns 〕 *n.* 堅持；堅毅

memory〔ˋmɛmərɪ〕 *n.* 記憶；回憶

The Persistence of Memory

enigma〔 ɪˋnɪgmə 〕 *n.* 難解的謎

project〔ˋprɑdʒɛkt〕 *n.* 計畫

stage〔 stedʒ 〕 *n.* 舞台

screen〔 skrin 〕 *n.* 螢幕

select〔 səˋlɛkt 〕 *v.* 挑選

program〔ˋprogræm〕 *n.* 節目

reflect〔 rɪˋflɛkt 〕 *v.* 反射；反映

L'Enigme sans Fin

showman〔ˋʃomən〕 *n.* 表演者

quality〔ˋkwɑlətɪ〕 *n.* 特質；特色

1. (**A**) What is Dali's *The Persistence of Memory* considered
　　　 to be? 達利的「記憶的堅持」被認為是什麼？

　　(A) One of his masterpieces. 他的傑作之一。

　　(B) One of the best TV programs.
　　　　最好的電視節目之一。

　　* consider〔 kənˋsɪdə 〕 *v.* 認為
　　　masterpiece〔ˋmæstə͵pis 〕 *n.* 傑作

TEST 81

【2015 高考福建卷】

Have you ever heard of the Stilton Cheese Rolling Festival? Teams of four, dressed in a variety of strange and funny clothes, roll a complete wooden cheese along a 50-meter course. On the way, they must not kick or throw their cheese, or go into their competitors' lane. The chief prize is a complete Stilton cheese weighing about four kilos.

1. In the Stilton cheese rolling competition, competitors on each team must _____.

   A. roll a wooden cheese in their own lane

   B. use a real cheese weighing about four kilos

TEST　82

【2015 高考全國卷】

More students than ever before are taking a gap year before going to university. It used to be called the "year off" between school and university. The gap-year phenomenon originated as the time between entrance exams in November and the start of the next academic year.

1. What do we learn about the gap year from the text?

A. It is increasingly popular.

B. It is required by universities.

TEST 81 詳解

【2015 高考福建卷】

Have you *ever* heard of the Stilton Cheese Rolling Festival? Teams *of four, dressed in a variety of strange **and** funny clothes*, roll a complete wooden cheese *along a 50-meter course. On the way*, they must not kick or throw their cheese, *or* go into their competitors' lane. The chief prize is a complete Stilton cheese *weighing about four kilos*.

你曾經聽說過「斯蒂爾頓滾乳酪大賽」嗎？每隊四人，穿著各式各樣奇怪好笑的衣服，沿著一條 50 公尺的賽道，滾動一個完全木製的乳酪。在途中，他們不可以踢或丟他們的乳酪，也不可以跑進他們對手的賽道。大獎是一塊完整的、重達大約四公斤的斯蒂爾頓乳酪。

* *hear of* 聽說
Stilton〔ˈstɪltn̩〕*n.* 斯蒂爾頓【英國地名，著名斯蒂爾頓乳酪產地】
cheese〔tʃiz〕*n.* 乳酪；起司   roll〔rol〕*v.* 滾動
festival〔ˈfɛstəvl̩〕*n.* 節日；慶典   team〔tim〕*n.* 隊伍
be dressed in 穿著   variety〔vəˈraɪətɪ〕*n.* 多樣性；變化
a variety of 各式各樣的   strange〔strendʒ〕*adj.* 奇怪的
funny〔ˈfʌnɪ〕*adj.* 滑稽的；好笑的
clothes〔kloz〕*n. pl.* 衣服
complete〔kəmˈplit〕*adj.* 完全的；完整的

wooden〔'wʊdṇ〕*adj.* 木頭的

along〔ə'lɔŋ〕*prep.* 沿著⋯　　meter〔'mitə〕*n.* 公尺；米

course〔kors〕*n.* 路線　***on the way*** 在途中

must not V 不可以【表禁止】　　kick〔kɪk〕*v.* 踢

throw〔θro〕*v.* 丟　　***go into*** 進入

competitor〔kəm'pɛtətə〕*n.* 對手；競爭者

lane〔len〕*n.* 線道　　chief〔tʃif〕*adj.* 最大的；主要的

prize〔praɪz〕*n.* 獎品；獎

weigh〔we〕*v.* 重達　　kilo〔'kɪlo〕*n.* 公斤

1. (**A**) In the Stilton cheese rolling competition, competitors
on each team must _____.

在「斯蒂爾頓滾乳酪大賽」中，每一隊的競爭者必須 _____。

(A) roll a wooden cheese in their own lane

<u>在他們自己的線道上滾動一個木製的乳酪</u>

(B) use a real cheese weighing about four kilos

使用重達大約四公斤的真正乳酪

* competition〔ˌkɑmpə'tɪʃən〕*n.* 競爭；比賽

real〔'riəl〕*adj.* 真的；真實的

TEST 82 詳解

【2015 高考全國卷】

More students *than ever before* are taking a gap year

before going to university. It used to be called the "year off" *between school and university.* The gap-year phenomenon

originated as the time *between entrance exams in November*

and the start of the next academic year.

　　在上大學之前休間隔年假期的學生，比以前更多了，它過去被稱爲中學和大學之間的「休息年」。間隔年的現象起源於，十一月的入學考試和下一個學年開始之間的時間。

> * gap〔gæp〕*n.* 間隔；空隙
> ***gap year*** 間隔年；空檔年【中學畢業後上大學前所休的一年
> 　　假期，通常用於旅遊或打工】
> university〔͵junə'vɝsətɪ〕*n.* 大學
> off〔ɔf〕*adv.* (工作、上學等) 休息
> phenomenon〔fə'nɑmə͵nɑn〕*n.* 現象
> originate〔ə'rɪdʒə͵net〕*v.* 起源於；開始
> entrance〔'ɛntrəns〕*n.* 入學
> academic〔͵ækə'dɛmɪk〕*adj.* 學術的
> ***academic year*** 學年 (= *school year*)

1. (**A**) What do we learn about the gap year from the text?
　　從本文中關於間隔年我們可以得知什麼？

　　(A) It is increasingly popular. 它逐漸在流行。

　　(B) It is required by universities. 它被大學所要求。

> * learn〔lɝn〕*v.* 得知　　text〔tɛkst〕*n.* 本文；正文
> increasingly〔ɪn'krisɪŋlɪ〕*adv.* 逐漸地
> popular〔'pɑpjələ〕*adj.* 受歡迎的
> require〔rɪ'kwaɪr〕*v.* 要求；需要

TEST 83

【2015 高考福建卷】

Papa, as a son of a dirt-poor farmer, left school early and went to work in a factory. So, the world became his school. He read everything he could lay his hands on. "There's so much to learn," he'd say. "Though we're born stupid, only the stupid remain that way." He was determined that none of his children would be denied an education.

1. What do we know from the paragraph?
   A. The author's father was born in a factory worker's family.
   B. The author's father thought highly of education.

TEST 84

【2015 高考全國卷】

"Psychology cafés", which offer great comfort, are among the most popular places in Paris. Middle-aged homemakers, retirees, and the unemployed come to such cafés to talk about love, anger, and dreams with a psychologist. "There's a strong need in Paris for communication," says a regular customer. "People have few real friends. And they need to open up."

1. Why are psychology cafés becoming popular in Paris?

   A. They give people emotional support.

   B. They offer a platform for business links.

TEST 83 詳解

【2015 高考福建卷】

Papa, *as a son of a dirt-poor farmer*, left school *early **and***

went to work *in a factory*. *So*, the world became his school.

He read everything *he could lay his hands on*. "There's so

much to learn," he'd say. "***Though** we're born stupid*, only

the stupid remain that way." He was determined ***that** none*

of his children would be denied an education.

　　爸爸是一個赤貧的農夫之子，很早就離開學校，到工廠工作。所以，這個世界就成爲他的學校。他閱讀他所能得到的每一樣東西。他常說：「要學習的東西這麼多。雖然我們出生時很愚蠢，但只有愚蠢的人會保持那個樣子。」他很堅決，他的小孩沒有人會被拒絕敎育的機會。

* dirt-poor〔'dɜt,pʊr〕*adj.* 非常貧窮的；赤貧的
  farmer〔'farmə〕*n.* 農夫　　factory〔'fæktrɪ〕*n.* 工廠
  lay hands on 拿住；抓住　　stupid〔'stupɪd〕*adj.* 愚蠢的
  remain〔rɪ'men〕*v.* 保持
  determined〔dɪ'tɜmɪnd〕*adj.* 堅決的
  none〔nʌn〕*pron.* 沒人；誰也沒有
  deny〔dɪ'naɪ〕*v.* 否認；拒絕給予
  education〔,ɛdʒə'keʃən〕*n.* 敎育

1.(**B**) What do we know from the paragraph?

從本段落我們知道什麼？

(A) The author's father was born in a factory worker's family.

作者的父親出生在一個工廠工人的家裡。

(B) The author's father thought highly of education.

作者的父親非常重視教育。

* paragraph〔'pærə,græf〕*n.* 段落

author〔'ɔθə〕*n.* 作者　　worker〔'wɜkə〕*n.* 工人

highly〔'haɪlɪ〕*adv.* 高度地　***think highly of*** 尊重；重視

TEST 84 詳解

【 **2015 高考全國卷** 】

"Psychology cafés", **which** *offer great comfort*, are among the most popular places *in Paris*. Middle-aged homemakers, retirees, **and** the unemployed come to such cafés *to talk about love, anger,* **and** *dreams with a psychologist*. "There's a strong need *in Paris for communication*," says a regular customer.

"People have few real friends. **And** they need to open up."

　　心理咖啡廳可以提供很大的慰藉，是巴黎最受歡迎的地方之一。中年主婦、退休者，還有失業的人，都會來這種咖啡廳，和心理學家談論愛情、憤怒和夢想。「在巴黎，有強烈的需求需要溝通，」一位常客說道，「人們眞正的朋友很少，而他們需要敞開心胸。」

　　* psychology〔saɪˋkɑlədʒɪ〕*n.* 心理學
　　café〔kəˋfe , kæˋfe〕*n.* 咖啡廳　　offer〔ˋɔfɚ〕*v.* 提供
　　comfort〔ˋkʌmfɚt〕*n.* 舒適；安慰
　　among〔əˋmʌŋ〕*prep.* 在～之中；是～之一
　　middle〔ˋmɪdḷ〕*adj.* 中間的　　***middle-aged*** *adj.* 中年的
　　homemaker〔ˋhomˏmekɚ〕*n.* 主婦（= *housewife*）；持家的人
　　retiree〔rɪˏtaɪˋri〕*n.* 退休者
　　unemployed〔ˏʌnɪmˋplɔɪd〕*adj.* 失業的
　　the unemployed 失業者　　***talk about*** 談論
　　psychologist〔saɪˋkɑlədʒɪst〕*n.* 心理學家
　　communication〔kəˏmjunəˋkeʃən〕*n.* 溝通
　　regular〔ˋrɛgjələ〕*adj.* 經常的
　　customer〔ˋkʌstəmɚ〕*n.* 顧客　　***open up*** 開放；敞開心胸

1. (**A**) Why are psychology cafés becoming popular in Paris?
　　　心理咖啡廳為何在巴黎越來越受歡迎？

　　(A) They give people emotional support.
　　　　他們給予人們情緒上的支持。

　　(B) They offer a platform for business links.
　　　　他們提供一個商業連結的平台。

　　* emotional〔ɪˋmoʃənḷ〕*adj.* 情緒的
　　　support〔səˋport〕*n.* 支持；支援
　　　platform〔ˋplætˏfɔrm〕*n.* 平台
　　　business〔ˋbɪznɪs〕*n.* 商業　　link〔lɪŋk〕*n.* 連結

TEST 85

【2015 高考全國卷】

The tour includes a guided tour of Windsor and Hampton Court, Henry VIII's favorite palace. With 500 years of history, Hampton Court was once the home of four Kings and one Queen. Now this former royal palace is open to the public as a major tourist attraction. Visit the palace and its various historic gardens, which include the famous maze.

1. Why is Hampton Court a major tourist attraction?
    A. It used to be the home of royal families.
    B. It used to be a well-known maze.

TEST 85 詳解

【2015 高考全國卷】

The tour includes a guided tour *of Windsor **and** Hampton*

Court, Henry VIII's favorite palace.　*With 500 years of history,*

Hampton Court was *once* the home *of four Kings **and** one*

Queen.　*Now* this former royal palace is open to the public *as*

a major tourist attraction.　Visit the palace and its various

historic gardens, ***which** include the famous maze.*

　　這個行程包含溫莎城堡和漢普敦宮的導覽旅行，這裡是亨利八世最喜歡的宮殿。漢普敦宮有五百年的歷史，曾經是四任國王和一任女王的家。現在，這座前王室宮殿已經開放給大眾參觀，是重要的觀光景點之一。來參觀這座宮殿，還有這裡各式各樣有歷史性的庭園，其中包括著名的迷宮。

> * include〔ɪn'klud〕*v.* 包括；包含
> guide〔gaɪd〕*v.* 引導；引領　　***guided tour*** 導覽旅行
> Windsor〔'wɪnzɚ〕*n.* 溫莎【此指溫莎城堡，是英國王室溫莎王朝的家族城堡】　　court〔kort〕*n.* 宮廷
> ***Hampton Court*** 漢普敦宮【是屬於英國王亨利八世的宮殿】
> ***Henry VIII*** 亨利八世【1491-1547，是英國都鐸王朝第二任國王，他推行英國的宗教改革，成立英國國教】

favorite〔'fevərit〕*adj.* 最喜愛的

palace〔'pælis〕*n.* 宮殿　　once〔wʌns〕*adv.* 曾經

queen〔kwin〕*n.* 王后；女王

former〔'fɔrmɚ〕*adj.* 前任的；以前的

royal〔'rɔɪəl〕*adj.* 王室的；皇家的

the public 大眾　　major〔'medʒɚ〕*adj.* 主要的；重要的

tourist〔'turist〕*adj.* 觀光的　　*n.* 觀光客

attraction〔ə'trækʃən〕*n.* 吸引人之物

tourist attraction 觀光景點　　visit〔'vizit〕*v.* 參觀；遊覽

various〔'vɛrɪəs〕*adj.* 各式各樣的

historic〔his'tɔrik〕*adj.* 有歷史性的

garden〔'gɑrdṇ〕*n.* 公園；庭園

famous〔'feməs〕*adj.* 有名的　　maze〔mez〕*n.* 迷宮

1. (**A**) Why is Hampton Court a major tourist attraction?

為什麼漢普敦宮是個主要的觀光景點？

(A) It used to be the home of royal families.

它以前是王室成員的家。

(B) It used to be a well-known maze.

它以前是著名的迷宮。

* well-known〔'wɛl'non〕*adj.* 著名的

TEST　86

【2015 高考福建卷】

Everyone knows that exercise is good for the body. However, when exercise is performed in groups, it's not only great for improving physical health but also psychological health. It's an opportunity to be social, release endorphins, and improve your strength. Additionally, group exercise creates a community feeling. The support that comes with taking on a fitness journey with others proves more effective than going to the gym alone.

1. The paragraph focuses on _____.

   A. the most effective way to improve physical fitness

   B. the contribution of group exercise to psychological health

TEST 86 詳解

【2015 高考福建卷】

名詞子句做受詞

Everyone knows ***that exercise is good for the body.***

However, ***when exercise is performed in groups,*** it's ***not only***

great *for improving physical health* ***but also*** psychological

health. It's an opportunity to be social, release endorphins,

and improve your strength. *Additionally*, group exercise

creates a community feeling. The support ***that comes with***

taking on a fitness journey with others proves more effective

than going to the gym alone.

　　每個人都知道，運動對身體有好處。然而，當團體一起做運動時，不只對改善身體健康有幫助，心理健康也是。這是一個社交、釋放腦內啡，和改善體力的機會。此外，團體運動創造一個群體感。與其他人一起進行健身之旅，所帶來的支持感，證明比自己上健身房更有效。

　　* perform〔 pɚˋfɔrm〕*v.* 表演；執行
　　　group〔 grup〕*n.* 群；團體
　　　improve〔 ɪmˋpruv〕*v.* 改善
　　　physical〔ˋfɪzɪkl̩〕*adj.* 身體的

health〔 hɛlθ 〕*n.* 健康；健全

psychological〔ˌsaɪkəˈlɑdʒɪkl̩〕*adj.* 心理的

opportunity〔ˌɑpɚˈtunətɪ〕*n.* 機會

social〔ˈsoʃəl〕*adj.* 社交的；社會的

release〔rɪˈlis〕*v.* 釋放；解放

endorphin〔ɛnˈdɔrfɪn〕*n.* 腦內啡【當運動量超過某一階段時，
　體內便會分泌腦內啡，使你覺得放鬆或精力充沛】

strength〔strɛŋ(k)θ〕*n.* 力量；體力

additionally〔əˈdɪʃənl̩ɪ〕*adv.* 此外

create〔krɪˈet〕*v.* 創造

community〔kəˈmjunətɪ〕*n.* 社區；社會

support〔səˈport〕*n.* 支持；支撐　　***take on*** 進行

fitness〔ˈfɪtnɪs〕*n.* 健康；健身

journey〔ˈdʒɝnɪ〕*n.* 旅程　　prove〔pruv〕*v.* 證明

effective〔əˈfɛktɪv〕*adj.* 有效的

gym〔dʒɪm〕*n.* 體育館；健身房

alone〔əˈlon〕*adv.* 獨自地

1. (**B**) The paragraph focuses on ＿＿＿＿＿.
　　本段落主要重點在 ＿＿＿＿＿。

　　(A) the most effective way to improve physical fitness
　　　改善身體健康最有效的方式

　　(B) the contribution of group exercise to psychological
　　　health　團體運動對心理健康的貢獻

　　* paragraph〔ˈpærəˌgræf〕*n.* 段落
　　　focus〔ˈfokəs〕*v.* 聚焦；專注 < *on* >
　　　contribution〔ˌkɑntrəˈbjuʃən〕*n.* 貢獻

TEST 87

【2015 高考重慶卷】

Shopkeepers can attract customers to their shops simply by making changes to the environment. One tactic involves where to display the goods. For example, stores place fruits and vegetables in the first section. They know that customers who buy the healthy food first will feel happy, and then they will buy more junk food later in their trip.

1. Why do stores usually display fruits and vegetables in the first section?

   A. To show they are high quality food.

   B. To help sell junk food.

TEST 88

【2015 高考四川卷】

Dad bought a small farm, planting vegetables and fruit trees. Every week he cleaned Old Man McColgin's chicken house in exchange for manure. When we complained about the terrible smell, Dad said the stronger the manure, the healthier the crops, and he was right. For example, one of his melons filled the entire house with its sweet smell, and the taste was even sweeter.

1. Why did Dad clean Old Man McColgin's chicken house regularly?

   A. To earn some money for the family.

   B. To collect manure for his crops.

TEST 87 詳解

【2015 高考重慶卷】

Shopkeepers can attract customers *to their shops simply by making changes to the environment.* One tactic involves **where** *to display the goods*. *For example*, stores place fruits
名詞片語做受詞

and vegetables *in the first section.* They know **that** *customers* **who** *buy the healthy food first will feel happy*, **and** *then they will buy more junk food later in their trip.*

商店老闆可以把顧客吸引到店裡來，僅僅藉由改變環境即可。有一項策略是關於商品的展示地點。例如，商店把水果和蔬菜放在第一區。他們知道，優先購買健康食物的顧客會覺得很滿意，然後當他們逛到後面時，就會買更多的垃圾食物。

* shopkeeper〔ˋʃɑpˏkipɚ〕*n.* 商店老闆 (= *storekeeper*)
  attract〔əˋtrækt〕*v.* 吸引
  customer〔ˋkʌstəmɚ〕*n.* 顧客；客戶
  simply〔ˋsɪmplɪ〕*adv.* 簡單地；僅僅
  environment〔ɪnˋvaɪrənmənt〕*n.* 環境
  tactic〔ˋtæktɪk〕*n.* 策略   involve〔ɪnˋvɑlv〕*v.* 牽涉；包含
  display〔dɪˋsple〕*v.* 展示；陳列
  goods〔gʊdz〕*n. pl.* 貨物；商品   **for example** 例如

place〔ples〕*v.* 放置（=*put*）

section〔'sɛkʃən〕*n.* 部分；地區

healthy〔'hɛlθɪ〕*adj.* 健康的　　junk〔dʒʌŋk〕*n.* 垃圾

junk food 垃圾食物　　later〔'letɚ〕*adv.* 隨後；後來

1. (**B**)　Why do stores usually display fruits and vegetables in
the first section?

　　爲什麼商店通常把水果和蔬菜展示在第一區？

　　(A) To show they are high quality food.

　　　　爲了展示它們是高品質的食物。

　　(B) To help sell junk food.　爲了幫助販賣垃圾食物。

　　* usually〔'juʒuəlɪ〕*adv.* 通常

　　　high〔haɪ〕*adj.* 高的　　quality〔'kwɑlətɪ〕*n.* 品質

TEST 88 詳解

【2015 高考四川卷】

　　Dad bought a small farm, *planting vegetables* **and** *fruit*

trees. Every week he cleaned Old Man McColgin's chicken

house *in exchange for manure.* ***When*** *we complained about*

the terrible smell, Dad said *the stronger the manure, the*

healthier the crops, **and** he was right. *For example,* one of his melons filled the entire house *with its sweet smell,* ***and***

the taste was *even* sweeter.

　　爸爸買了一座小農場，種了蔬菜和果樹。他每週會去清理麥考金老人的雞舍，以交換肥料。當我們抱怨肥料的臭味時，爸爸說，肥料的味道越重，農作物就會越健康，而他說的是對的。例如，他的一顆甜瓜，讓整個房子充滿了香甜的氣味，而吃起來的味道更甜。

* plant〔plænt〕*v.* 種植；栽種
  McColgin〔mæk'kɑldʒɪn〕*n.* 麥考金【姓氏】
  exchange〔ɪks'tʃendʒ〕*n.* 交換
  in exchange for… 以交換…
  manure〔mə'njʊr〕*n.* 肥料；糞肥
  complain〔kəm'plen〕*v.* 抱怨 <*about, of* >
  terrible〔'tɛrəbḷ〕*adj.* 糟糕的；駭人的
  smell〔smɛl〕*n.* 氣味　　crop〔krɑp〕*n.* 農作物
  melon〔'mɛlən〕*n.* 甜瓜　　fill〔fɪl〕*v.* 裝滿；使充滿 <*with* >
  entire〔ɪn'taɪr〕*adj.* 整個的　　taste〔test〕*n.* (吃起來的)味道

1. (**B**) Why did Dad clean Old Man McColgin's chicken house regularly?
   為什麼爸爸要定期清理麥考金老人的雞舍？
   (A) To earn some money for the family.
   　　為了為家裡賺一些錢。
   (B) To collect manure for his crops.
   　　為了為他的農作物收集肥料。

   * regularly〔'rɛgjələlɪ〕*adv.* 定期地；經常地
     earn〔ɝn〕*v.* 賺(錢)　　collect〔kə'lɛkt〕*v.* 收集；蒐集

TEST 89

【2015 高考重慶卷】

Some works of art can excite the human mind across cultures and through centuries. In 1757, a philosopher argued that it is because "the general principles of taste are uniform in human nature." He observed that Homer was still admired after two thousand years. Works of this type, he believed, have timeless appeal and will probably be enjoyed for centuries into the future.

1. According to the philosopher, some works of art can exist for centuries because

   A. they establish some general principles of art.

   B. they appeal to unchanging features of human nature.

TEST 89 詳解

【2015 高考重慶卷】

Some works of art can excite the human mind *across cultures **and** through centuries.* In 1757, a philosopher argued **that** it is **because** "*the general principles of taste are uniform in human nature.*" He observed **that** *Homer was still admired after two thousand years.* Works *of this type, he believed,* have timeless appeal **and** will *probably* be enjoyed *for centuries into the future.*

　　有些藝術作品可以激勵人心，而且跨越文化、橫亙數世紀。在 1757 年，有一位哲學家主張，那是因為在人類的天性裡，對品味的一般原則是一致的。他觀察到，荷馬在二千年後仍然受人讚嘆。他相信。這種類型的作品有永恆的魅力，可能在未來數個世紀，還是會受人喜愛。

　　* work〔wɝk〕*n.* 作品　　art〔ɑrt〕*n.* 藝術
　　　excite〔ɪkˈsaɪt〕*v.* 刺激；使興奮
　　　human〔ˈhjumən〕*adj.* 人的；人類的
　　　mind〔maɪnd〕*n.* 心；精神
　　　across〔əˈkrɔs〕*prep.* 橫越；跨越
　　　culture〔ˈkʌltʃɚ〕*n.* 文化

through〔θru〕 *prep.* 穿過；整個期間

century〔'sɛntʃərɪ〕 *n.* 世紀

philosopher〔fə'lasəfə 〕 *n.* 哲學家

argue〔'argju〕 *v.* 爭論；主張

general〔'dʒɛnərəl〕 *adj.* 一般的；普通的

principle〔'prɪnsəpl̩〕 *n.* 原則；原理

taste〔test〕 *n.* 品味；喜好

uniform〔'junə,fɔrm〕 *adj.* 一致的；相同的

nature〔'netʃə 〕 *n.* 自然；天性　　observe〔əb'zɝv〕 *v.* 觀察

Homer〔'homə 〕 *n.* 荷馬【古希臘吟遊詩人，史詩《伊里亞德》

（the Iliad）和《奧德賽》（the Odyssey）的創作者】

admire〔əd'maɪr〕 *v.* 欽佩；讚賞　　type〔taɪp〕 *n.* 種類

timeless〔'taɪmlɪs〕 *adj.* 無窮的；永恆的

appeal〔ə'pil〕 *n.* 吸引力；魅力

probably〔'prabəblɪ〕 *adv.* 可能　　future〔'fjutʃə 〕 *n.* 未來

1. (**B**) According to the philosopher, some works of art can
exist for centuries because
根據這位哲學家的說法，有些藝術品可以存在數世紀，是因為

(A) they establish some general principles of art.
它們建立了一些藝術的一般原則。

(B) they appeal to unchanging features of human nature.
它們吸引了人性不變的特色。

* exist〔ɪg'zɪst〕 *v.* 存在
establish〔ə'stæblɪʃ〕 *v.* 建立　　***appeal to*** 吸引
unchanging〔ʌn'tʃendʒɪŋ〕 *adj.* 不變的
feature〔'fitʃə 〕 *n.* 特徵；特色

TEST 90

【2015 高考重慶卷】

When you go on safari on horseback, the guides take you to beautiful shallow lakes full of water lilies. Rainbows form in the splashing water around you. You are very likely to come across large wild animals, too. On horseback it is possible to get quite close to elephants, giraffes, and many other animals. It is truly exciting.

1. What does the author find most exciting about a horseback safari?

   A. Hunting large animals just as our ancestors did.

   B. Being part of the scene and getting close to animals.

TEST　91

【2015 高考北京卷】

Transparent animals let light pass through their bodies. These animals typically live between the surface of the ocean and a depth of about 3,300 feet—as far as most light can reach. Most of them are extremely delicate and can be damaged by a simple touch. These animals live through their life alone. They never touch anything unless they're eating it, or unless something is eating them.

1. According to the paragraph, transparent animals _____.

　A. can be easily damaged

　B. appear only in the deep ocean

TEST 90 詳解

【2015 高考重慶卷】

***When** you go on safari on horseback*, the guides take you to beautiful shallow lakes *full of water lilies*. Rainbows form *in the splashing water around you*. You are *very* likely to come across large wild animals, *too*. *On horseback* <u>it</u> is

虛主詞

possible [to get *quite* close to elephants, giraffes, ***and*** many

真正主詞

other animals.] It is *truly* exciting.

　　當你騎著馬做狩獵旅行時，嚮導們會帶你去很美的淺水湖泊，上面充滿著睡蓮。彩虹在你周圍飛濺的水中形成。你也非常有可能會遇見大型的野生動物。騎在馬背上，有可能相當接近大象、長頸鹿，和其他許多動物。真是非常地刺激。

* safari〔səˋfɑrɪ〕*n.* 狩獵旅行　　***go on (a) safari*** 去狩獵旅行
  horseback〔ˋhɔrs͵bæk〕*n.* 馬背
  on horseback 騎馬；騎在馬背上
  guide〔gaɪd〕*n.* 導遊；嚮導　　shallow〔ˋʃælo〕*adj.* 淺的
  lake〔lek〕*n.* 湖　　***be full of*** 充滿
  lily〔ˋlɪlɪ〕*n.* 百合；百合花　　***water lily*** 睡蓮
  rainbow〔ˋren͵bo〕*n.* 彩虹　　form〔fɔrm〕*v.* 形成

splash〔splæʃ〕v. 濺；飛濺　　***be likely to V*** 可能

come across 偶遇　　wild〔waɪld〕adj. 野生的

quite〔kwaɪt〕adv. 相當地　　close〔klos〕adj. 接近的＜ to ＞

giraffe〔dʒəˈræf〕n. 長頸鹿

truly〔ˈtrulɪ〕adv. 真實地；真正地

exciting〔ɪkˈsaɪtɪŋ〕adj. 刺激的；令人興奮的

1. (**B**) What does the author find most exciting about
a horseback safari?

　　關於騎馬狩獵，作者覺得最刺激的是什麼？

　　(A) Hunting large animals just as our ancestors did.

　　　　獵取大型動物，就像我們祖先所做的。

　　(B) Being part of the scene and getting close to animals.

　　　　融入景色並接近動物。

　　* author〔ˈɔθɚ〕n. 作者　　hunt〔hʌnt〕v. 狩獵；獵取
　　　ancestor〔ˈænsɛstɚ〕n. 祖先　　scene〔sin〕n. 風景；背景

TEST 91 詳解

【 2016 高考北京卷 】

Transparent animals let light pass *through their bodies*.

These animals *typically* live ***between*** *the surface of the ocean*

and *a depth of about 3,300 feet*—*as far **as** most light can reach*.

Most of them are *extremely* delicate ***and*** can be damaged *by* *a simple touch.* These animals live *through their life alone.*

They never touch anything **unless they're eating it, or unless**

something is eating them.

　　透明的動物能讓光線通過牠們的身體。這些動物通常住在海洋表面和大約 3,300 英呎的深度之間，這是大部分的光可達到的最遠處。牠們絕大多數都非常脆弱，碰一下可能就會受傷。這些動物終其一生都是獨居的。牠們從不接觸任何生物，除非是牠們正在吃這個生物，或是這個生物正在吃牠們。

* transparent〔træns'pɛrənt〕*adj.* 透明的
　let〔lɛt〕*v.* 允許；讓　　pass〔pæs〕*v.* 通過；經過
　through〔θru〕*prep.* 通過；經過；整個期間
　body〔'bɑdɪ〕*n.* 身體；軀體
　typically〔'tɪpɪk!ɪ〕*adv.* 典型地；通常
　surface〔'sɝfɪs〕*n.* 表面　　ocean〔'oʃən〕*n.* 海洋
　depth〔dɛpθ〕*n.* 深；深度
　foot〔fut〕*n.* 英呎【複數形為 feet〔fit〕】
　reach〔ritʃ〕*v.* 到達；抵達
　extremely〔ɪk'strimlɪ〕*adv.* 非常地；極度地
　delicate〔'dɛləkət〕*adj.* 脆弱的；柔弱的
　damage〔'dæmɪdʒ〕*v.* 損傷　　simple〔'sɪmp!〕*adj.* 簡單的
　touch〔tʌtʃ〕*n., v.* 碰觸；接觸　　unless〔ən'lɛs〕*conj.* 除非

1. (**A**) According to the paragraph, transparent animals ＿＿＿＿.
　　根據本段，透明的動物 ＿＿＿＿＿。
　　(A) can be easily damaged 很容易受到損傷
　　(B) appear only in the deep ocean 只出現在深海中
　　* appear〔ə'pɪr〕*v.* 出現　　deep〔dip〕*adj.* 深的

TEST 92

【2015 高考天津卷】

The Jibo robot is designed to be a personalized assistant. You can talk to it, ask it questions, and make requests for it to perform different tasks. It doesn't just deliver general answers to questions; it responds based on what it learns about each individual in the household. It can do things such as reminding an elderly family member to take medicine or taking family photos.

1. What can a Jibo robot do according to the paragraph?

   A. Answer your questions and make requests.

   B. Obey your orders and remind you to take pills.

TEST 93

【2015 高考浙江卷】

From the very beginning of school we make books and reading a constant source of possible failure and public humiliation. We make children read aloud before others so that we can be sure they "know" all the words they are reading. This means that when they don't know a word, they are going to make a mistake, right in front of everyone. It is no wonder so many children dislike reading.

1. According to the passage, children's fear and dislike of books may result from

    A. being made to read too much.

    B. being made to read aloud before others.

TEST 92 詳解

【2015 高考天津卷】

The Jibo robot is designed *to be a personalized assistant.*
You can talk to it, ask it questions, ***and*** make requests *for it to perform different tasks.* It doesn't *just* deliver general answers *to questions*; it responds *based on **what** it learns about each individual in the household.* It can do things *such as reminding an elderly family member to take medicine **or** taking family photos.*

　　Jibo 機器人被設計成個人化助理。你可以和它說話、問它問題，還可以做出要求，讓它去執行不同的工作。它不只會答出各種問題的一般答案，它還會根據它所學習到的家裡每一個人的資料作回應。它可以做一些事情，像是提醒家裡的長者吃藥，或拍家庭照。

* robot〔'robɑt〕 n. 機器人　　design〔dɪ'zaɪn〕 v. 設計
personalized〔'pɝsṇḷ͵aɪzd〕 adj. 個人化的
assistant〔ə'sɪstənt〕 n. 助手；助理
request〔rɪ'kwɛst〕 n. 要求
perform〔pɚ'fɔrm〕 v. 做；執行
task〔tæsk〕 n. 任務；工作
deliver〔dɪ'lɪvɚ〕 v. 遞交；給予；實現
general〔'dʒɛnərəl〕 adj. 一般的；普遍的

respond〔rɪˋspɑnd〕v. 回答；回應　***based on***　根據
individual〔͵ɪndəˋvɪdʒʊəl〕n. 個人
household〔ˋhaʊs͵hold〕n. 家族；家庭
remind〔rɪˋmaɪnd〕v. 提醒
elderly〔ˋɛldɚlɪ〕adj. 有相當年紀的；年長的
family member　家庭成員；家人
take medicine　吃藥　　***take photos***　拍照

1.(**B**) What can a Jibo robot do according to the paragraph?
根據本段，Jibo 機器人可以做什麼？

(A) Answer your questions and make requests.
回答你的問題，做出要求。

(B) Obey your orders and remind you to take pills.
<u>服從你的命令，提醒你吃藥。</u>

* paragraph〔ˋpærə͵græf〕n. 段落　　obey〔əˋbe〕v. 服從
order〔ˋɔrdɚ〕n. 命令；指令　　pill〔pɪl〕n. 藥丸

TEST 93 詳解

【2015 高考浙江卷】

From the very beginning of school we make <u>books **and**</u>

<u>reading</u> a constant source *of possible failure **and** public*

humiliation. We make children read *aloud before others **so***

***that** we can be sure they "know" all the words they are reading.*

This means ***that when*** *they don't know a word*, they are going

to make a mistake, *right in front of everyone.* It is no wonder

so many children dislike reading.

　　從上學一開始，我們就使書本和閱讀成爲，不斷產生可能的恐懼和公開差辱的來源。我們要孩子們在其他人面前大聲閱讀，爲了確定他們「認識」他們讀的所有單字。這意味著，當他們不認識一個字時，他們將會犯錯，就在每一個人面前。難怪這麼多孩子不喜歡閱讀。

* constant〔'kɑnstənt〕*adj.* 不變的；一定的
  source〔sors〕*n.* 根源；來源　　failure〔'feljɚ〕*n.* 失敗
  public〔'pʌblɪk〕*adj.* 大衆的；公共的
  humiliation〔hju,mɪlɪ'eʃən〕*n.* 恥辱；差辱
  so that 爲了；以便【表目的的連接詞】
  aloud〔ə'laʊd〕*adv.* 出聲地；大聲地
  mean〔min〕*v.* 意謂；意指　　mistake〔mə'stek〕*n.* 錯誤
  front〔frʌnt〕*n.* 前面　　***in front of*** 在～前面
  wonder〔'wʌndɚ〕*n.* 神奇的東西；奇蹟
  no wonder 難怪　　dislike〔dɪs'laɪk〕*v.* 不喜歡

1. (**B**) According to the passage, children's fear and dislike of books may result from
   根據本文，孩子們對書本的恐懼和不喜歡，可能起因於
   (A) being made to read too much. 被強迫閱讀太多書。
   (B) being made to read aloud before others.
   　　被強迫在其他人面前大聲閱讀。

* passage〔'pæsɪdʒ〕*n.* 一段（文章）
  fear〔fɪr〕*n.* 恐懼　　***result from*** 起因於

TEST 94

【2015 高考安徽卷】

There are an extremely large number of ants worldwide. Each individual ant hardly weighs anything, but put together they weigh roughly the same as all of mankind. They also live nearly everywhere, except on frozen mountaintops and around the poles. For animals their size, ants have been astonishingly successful, largely due to their wonderful social behavior.

1. We can learn from the passage that ants are _____.

    A. not found around the poles

    B. too many to achieve any level of organization

TEST 94 詳解

【2015 高考安徽卷】

There are an *extremely* large number of ants *worldwide*.

Each individual ant *hardly* weighs anything, **but** *put together*

they *weigh roughly the same as all of mankind.* They *also* live

nearly everywhere, except on frozen mountaintops **and** *around*

the poles. *For animals their size*, ants have been *astonishingly*

successful, *largely due to their wonderful social behavior.*

　　全世界有非常多的螞蟻。個別的一隻螞蟻幾乎沒有重量，但是全部的螞蟻集合在一起，重量約略和全人類一樣重。此外，螞蟻幾乎在任何地方都能生存，除了冰凍的山頂和極地附近之外。以牠們這種體型的動物而言，螞蟻算是非常成功的，主要是由於牠們高度的社會化行為。

* extremely〔ɪk'strimlɪ〕*adv.* 非常地
  a large number of 很多；大量　　ant〔ænt〕*n.* 螞蟻
  worldwide〔'wɜld,waɪd〕*adv.* 全世界
  individual〔,ɪndə'vɪdʒʊəl〕*adj.* 個別的；單獨的
  hardly〔'hɑrdlɪ〕*adv.* 幾乎不
  weigh〔we〕*v.* 重達…
  put together 集合在一起
  roughly〔'rʌflɪ〕*adv.* 約略地

mankind〔mæn'kaɪnd〕*n.* 人類

nearly〔'nɪrlɪ〕*adv.* 幾乎；將近

except〔ɪk'sɛpt〕*prep.* 除了…之外

frozen〔'frozn̩〕*adj.* 結冰的；極冷的

mountaintop〔'maʊntn̩ˌtɑp〕*n.* 山頂

around〔ə'raʊnd〕*prep.* 在～附近　　pole〔pol〕*n.* 極地

astonishingly〔ə'stɑnɪʃɪŋlɪ〕*adv.* 驚人地；令人驚訝地

successful〔sək'sɛsfəl〕*adj.* 成功的

largely〔'lɑrdʒlɪ〕*adv.* 主要地　　*due to* 因為；由於

wonderful〔'wʌndəfəl〕*adj.* 不可思議的；極好的

social〔'soʃəl〕*adj.* 社會化的；社交的

behavior〔bɪ'hevjə〕*n.* 行為；舉止

1. (**A**) We can learn from the passage that ants are _____.

從本文我們可以得知，螞蟻 _____。

(A) not found around the poles

　　在極地附近找不到

(B) too many to achieve any level of organization

　　數量太多，而無法達成任何程度的組織化

* learn〔lɜn〕*v.* 得知

passage〔'pæsɪdʒ〕*n.* 一段（文章）

too ~ to V 太～而不…　　achieve〔ə'tʃiv〕*v.* 達到

level〔'lɛvl̩〕*n.* 水準；程度

organization〔ˌɔrgənə'zeʃən〕*n.* 組織

TEST 95

【2015 高考安徽卷】

Food serves as a form of communication. Sharing bread or other food is a common human tradition that can promote unity and trust. Food can also have a specific meaning, and play a significant role in celebrations or traditions. The foods we eat—and when and how we eat them—are often unique to a culture or may differ between rural and urban areas.

1. According to the passage, sharing bread
_____.

   A. can help to develop unity

   B. is a custom unique to rural areas

TEST 95 詳解

【2015 高考安徽卷】

Food serves as a form *of communication.* Sharing bread
主詞

or other food is a common human tradition *that can promote*

unity and trust. Food can *also* have a specific meaning, *and*

play a significant role *in celebrations or traditions.* The foods

we eat—and when and how we eat them—are *often* unique to

a culture *or* may differ *between rural and urban areas.*

食物可以作爲一種溝通的方式。分享麵包或其他食物，是一個很普遍的人類傳統，可以促進團結和信任。食物也可能有特定的意義，在慶祝活動或傳統中扮演重要的角色。我們所吃的食物——我們何時吃以及如何吃——常常都是每個文化特有的，而且在鄉村和都市地區也可能有所不同。

* ***serve as*** 擔任；當作　　form〔fɔrm〕*n.* 形式；方式
communication〔kə͵mjunə'keʃən〕*n.* 溝通
share〔ʃɛr〕*v.* 共享；分享　　bread〔brɛd〕*n.* 麵包
common〔'kɑmən〕*adj.* 一般的；常見的
human〔'hjumən〕*adj.* 人類的
tradition〔trə'dıʃən〕*n.* 傳統

promote〔prəˊmot〕*v.* 促進；增進

unity〔ˊjunətɪ〕*n.* 一致；和諧；團結

trust〔trʌst〕*n.* 信任

specific〔spɪˊsɪfɪk〕*adj.* 明確的

meaning〔ˊminɪŋ〕*n.* 意思；意義

significant〔sɪgˊnɪfəkənt〕*adj.* 重要的；重大的

role〔rol〕*n.* 角色（= *part*）

play a…role/part in~ 在～當中扮演一個…角色

celebration〔͵sɛləˊbreʃən〕*n.* 慶祝

unique〔juˊnik〕*adj.* 獨特的；特有的 *< to >*

culture〔ˊkʌltʃɚ〕*n.* 文化

differ〔ˊdɪfɚ〕*v.* 不同；有差異

rural〔ˊrurəl〕*adj.* 鄉下的；鄉村的

urban〔ˊɝbən〕*adj.* 都市的　　area〔ˊɛrɪə〕*n.* 地區

1. (**A**) According to the passage, sharing bread ＿＿＿＿＿.

　　根據本文，分享麵包 ＿＿＿＿＿。

　　(A) can help to develop unity

　　　　可以有助於團結的發展

　　(B) is a custom unique to rural areas

　　　　是一個鄉村地區特有的習俗

　　＊ passage〔ˊpæsɪdʒ〕*n.* 一段（文章）

　　　develop〔dɪˊvɛləp〕*v.* 發展

　　　custom〔ˊkʌstəm〕*n.* 風俗；習俗

TEST 96

【2015 高考湖北卷】

Hilversum is a medium-sized city in Holland. Unlike most of the Netherlands, Hilversum is actually in a hilly area with the soil mostly consisting of sand. Once called the Garden of Amsterdam, it still attracts travelers to come over to cycle and walk through the surrounding forests. They visit it for a relaxing day off the urban madness.

1. Hilversum is different from most of the Netherlands in that _____.

   A. it has a large population

   B. it is in a hilly area with sandy soil

TEST 96 詳解

【2015 高考湖北卷】

Hilversum is a medium-sized city *in Holland. Unlike most of the Netherlands*, Hilversum is actually in a hilly area *with the soil mostly consisting of sand.* Once called the *Garden of Amsterdam*, it *still* attracts travelers to come over to cycle and walk *through the surrounding forests.* They visit it *for a relaxing day off the urban madness.*

希爾弗瑟姆是荷蘭一個中型城市。不像荷蘭大部分地方，希爾弗瑟姆實際上位於一個丘陵地區，土壤多半是沙土。這裡曾經被稱爲「阿姆斯特丹的花園」，現在仍然吸引遊客到來，騎腳踏車或步行穿越周圍的森林。他們造訪此地，度過輕鬆的一天，以逃離都市的瘋狂。

* Hilversum〔ˈhɪlvəˌsəm〕*n.* 希爾弗瑟姆【位於荷蘭北部一城市】
  medium-sized〔ˈmidɪəmˌsaɪzd〕*adj.* 中型的；中號的
  Holland〔ˈhɑlənd〕*n.* 荷蘭【位於歐洲西北部，正式名稱爲 the kingdom of the Netherlands〔ˈnɛðələndz〕，首都阿姆斯特丹（Amsterdam〔ˈæmstəˌdæm〕），形容詞爲 Dutch〔dʌtʃ〕】
  unlike〔ʌnˈlaɪk〕*prep.* 不像
  actually〔ˈæktʃʊəlɪ〕*adv.* 實際上；實際地
  hilly〔ˈhɪlɪ〕*adj.* 多丘陵的　　area〔ˈɛrɪə〕*n.* 地區

soil〔sɔɪl〕*n.* 土；土壤　　mostly〔'mostlɪ〕*adv.* 多牛
consist〔kən'sɪst〕*v.* 組成＜*of*＞
sand〔sænd〕*n.* 沙　　once〔wʌns〕*adv.* 曾經；從前
garden〔'gardn〕*n.* 花園；公園
attract〔ə'trækt〕*v.* 吸引　　traveler〔'trævlɚ〕*n.* 旅客
cycle〔'saɪkḷ〕*v.* 騎腳踏車　　through〔θru〕*prep.* 穿過
surrounding〔sə'raʊndɪŋ〕*adj.* 周圍的
forest〔'fɔrɪst〕*n.* 森林　　visit〔'vɪzɪt〕*v.* 參觀；拜訪
relaxing〔rɪ'læksɪŋ〕*adj.* 令人放鬆的
off〔ɔf〕*prep.* 脫離；離開　　urban〔'ɝbən〕*adj.* 都市的
madness〔'mædnɪs〕*n.* 瘋狂；狂熱

1. (**B**) Hilversum is different from most of the Netherlands in
　　　that _____.

　　　希爾弗瑟姆和大部分荷蘭地區不同，在於 _____。

　　　(A) it has a large population

　　　　　它人口很多

　　　(B) it is in a hilly area with sandy soil

　　　　　它位於丘陵地區，有砂質土壤

　　　* *be different from* 和～不同

　　　　in that 在這一點上；因為；由於

　　　　population〔ˌpɑpjə'leʃən〕*n.* 人口

　　　　sandy〔'sændɪ〕*adj.* 沙質的；沙地的

TEST 97

【2015 高考湖北卷】

Space travel can be invisibly dangerous. For instance, astronauts lose bone mass. That's why exercise is considered extremely vital. The focus on fitness is as much about science and the future as it is about keeping any individual astronaut healthy. NASA is worried how astronauts can maintain strength and fitness for the long time in space.

1. One of NASA's major concerns about astronauts is
   A. how much exercise they do on the station.
   B. how they can remain healthy in space for a long time.

TEST 97 詳解

【 2015 高考湖北卷 】

Space travel can be *invisibly* dangerous. *For instance,*
astronauts lose bone mass. That's **why** *exercise is considered*
extremely vital. The focus *on fitness* is *as* much about science
and the future **as** *it is about keeping any individual astronaut*
healthy. NASA is worried **how** *astronauts can maintain*
strength **and** *fitness for the long time in space.*

　　太空旅行可能有看不見的危險。例如,太空人會骨質流失,那就是
為什麼運動被認為極為重要。強調健身對於保持任何一位太空人的健
康,和對於科學與未來一樣重要。太空總署擔憂,太空人長時間待在太
空中如何才能維持體力和健康。

* space〔spes〕*n.* 太空　　travel〔'trævl〕*n.* 旅行
  invisibly〔ɪn'vɪzəblɪ〕*adv.* 看不見地;隱藏地
  dangerous〔'dendʒərəs〕*adj.* 危險的
  for instance 例如 (= *for example*)
  astronaut〔'æstrə,nɔt〕*n.* 太空人
  lose〔luz〕*v.* 喪失;失去　　bone〔bon〕*n.* 骨頭
  mass〔mæs〕*n.* 質量　　***bone mass*** 骨質
  consider〔kən'sɪdə〕*v.* 認為
  extremely〔ɪk'strimlɪ〕*adv.* 非常地;極度地

vital〔'vaɪtl̩〕*adj.* 極為重要的

focus〔'fokəs〕*n.* 焦點；中心

fitness〔'fɪtnɪs〕*n.* 健康；健身　　future〔'fjutʃɚ〕*n.* 未來

individual〔ˌɪndə'vɪdʒuəl〕*adj.* 個別的；單獨的

healthy〔'hɛlθɪ〕*adj.* 健康的

NASA〔'næsə〕*n.* （美國）航空及太空總署（= *National Aeronautics and Space Administration*）

worried〔'wɜɪd〕*adj.* 擔心的；憂慮的

maintain〔men'ten〕*v.* 保持；維持

strength〔strɛŋ(k)θ〕*n.* 力量；體力

1.（**B**）One of NASA's major concerns about astronauts is
關於太空人，太空總署主要關心的事之一是

(A) how much exercise they do on the station.
他們在太空站上做了多少運動。

(B) how they can remain healthy in space for a long time.
他們在太空中如何才能長期保持健康。

* major〔'medʒɚ〕*adj.* 主要的

concern〔kən'sɜn〕*n.* 關心的事

station〔'steʃən〕*n.* 站；太空站

remain〔rɪ'men〕*v.* 保持；仍然

TEST 98

【2015 高考四川卷】

Robins are in danger of wearing themselves out by singing too much. They sing all night—as well as during the day. Researchers said that light from street lamps, takeaway signs and homes is affecting the birds' biological clocks, resulting in them being wide awake when they should be asleep. Lack of sleep could put the birds' health at risk.

1. According to researchers, what causes robins to sing so much?

   A. The light in modern life.

   B. The dangerous environment.

TEST 98 詳解

【2015 高考四川卷】

Robins are in danger of wearing themselves out *by*
singing too much. They sing *all night*—***as well as*** *during the*
day. Researchers said ***that*** *light from street lamps, takeaway*
signs ***and*** *homes is affecting the birds' biological clocks,*
resulting in them being wide awake ***when*** *they should be*
asleep. Lack of sleep could put the birds' health at risk.

　　知更鳥有危險了，牠們會因為一直唱歌，把自己累壞了。牠們整晚都在唱——白天也在唱。研究人員說，來自街燈、外賣食物的招牌和住家的燈光，正影響到知更鳥的生物時鐘，導致牠們應該睡覺的時間還是完全清醒的。缺乏睡眠可能將知更鳥的健康置於危險之中。

* robin〔'rɑbɪn〕*n.* 知更鳥　　danger〔'dendʒɚ〕*n.* 危險
  in danger of 有～危險
  wear out 磨損；使疲倦（*= exhaust*）
  during〔'durɪŋ〕*prep.* 在…期間
  researcher〔rɪ's3tʃɚ〕*n.* 研究人員
  light〔laɪt〕*n.* 光；光線
  lamp〔læmp〕*n.* 燈
  takeaway〔'tekə͵we〕*adj.* 外賣的（*= takeout*）

sign〔saɪn〕*n.* 標誌;告示;招牌　　affect〔əˈfɛkt〕*v.* 影響
biological〔ˌbaɪəˈlɑdʒɪkl〕*adj.* 生物(學)的
biological clock　生物時鐘
result in　導致;引起(= *cause*)
wide〔waɪd〕*adv.* 張大地;充分張開地
awake〔əˈwek〕*adj.* 醒的;醒著的
wide awake　完全清醒　　asleep〔əˈslip〕*adj.* 睡著的
lack〔læk〕*n.* 缺乏;缺少　　health〔hɛlθ〕*n.* 健康
risk〔rɪsk〕*n.* 風險;危險(= *danger*)
at risk　在危險中(= *in danger*)

1. (**A**) According to researchers, what causes robins to sing
so much?
根據研究人員的說法,什麼原因造成知更鳥一直唱歌?

(A) The light in modern life. 在現代生活的燈光。

(B) The dangerous environment. 危險的環境。

* cause〔kɔz〕*v.* 造成
modern〔ˈmɑdən〕*adj.* 現代的
dangerous〔ˈdendʒərəs〕*adj.* 危險的
environment〔ɪnˈvaɪrənmənt〕*n.* 環境

TEST 99

【2015 高考天津卷】

Boldness means a decision to <u>bite off more than you are sure you can eat</u>. And there is nothing mysterious about the mighty forces. They are potential powers we possess: energy, skill, sound judgment, creative ideas—even physical strength greater than most of us realize.

1. What is the implied meaning of the underlined part?

   A. Swallow more than you can digest.

   B. Act slightly above your abilities.

TEST 99 詳解

【2015 高考天津卷】

Boldness means a decision *to bite off more **than you are sure you can eat**.* ***And*** there is nothing mysterious *about the mighty forces*. They are potential powers *we possess*: energy, skill, sound judgment, creative ideas—*even physical strength greater **than** most of us realize*.

　　勇敢意指一種決定，要做得比你的能力多一點。關於那些強大的力量，沒有什麼神秘的，它們就是我們具有的潛在力量：精力、技巧、正確的判斷力、創意——甚至連體力都比我們所理解的更強大。

　　* boldness〔'boldnɪs〕*n.* 大膽；勇敢
　　mean〔min〕*v.* 意指　　decision〔dɪ'sɪʒən〕*n.* 決定
　　bite〔baɪt〕*v.* 咬下；咬掉 < *off* >
　　bite off more than you are sure you can eat 字面意思是「咬下比你確定你吃得下的多一些」，引申為「做得比你的能力多一點」，這句話改編自 bite off more than you can chew「咬下超過你嚼得動的；貪多嚼不爛；自不量力」。
　　mysterious〔mɪs'tɪrɪəs〕*adj.* 神秘的；不可思議的
　　mighty〔'maɪtɪ〕*adj.* 有力的；強大的
　　force〔fors〕*n.* 力量　　potential〔pə'tɛnʃəl〕*adj.* 潛在的

power〔'pauɚ〕*n.* 力量　　possess〔pə'zɛs〕*v.* 擁有；具有

energy〔'ɛnɚdʒɪ〕*n.* 精力；活力

skill〔skɪl〕*n.* 技巧；本領

sound〔saʊnd〕*adj.* 正常的；正確的

judgment〔'dʒʌdʒmənt〕*n.* 判斷

creative〔krɪ'etɪv〕*adj.* 獨創的；有創造力的

idea〔aɪ'diə〕*n.* 主意；構想

physical〔'fɪzɪkl̩〕*adj.* 身體的

strength〔strɛŋ(k)θ〕*n.* 力量；體力

realize〔'rɪə,laɪz〕*v.* 了解；理解

1. (**B**) What is the implied meaning of the underlined part?

　　畫線部分暗示什麼意思？

　　(A) Swallow more than you can digest.

　　　　吞下超過你可以消化的食物。

　　(B) Act slightly above your abilities.

　　　　<u>表現得比你的能力稍微超過一點。</u>

　　* imply〔ɪm'plaɪ〕*v.* 暗示　　meaning〔'minɪŋ〕*n.* 意思

　　　underline〔,ʌndɚ'laɪn〕*v.* 畫底線

　　　swallow〔'swɑlo〕*v.* 吞下；嚥下

　　　digest〔daɪ'dʒɛst〕*v.* 消化；消化食物

　　　act〔ækt〕*v.* 表現；行為

　　　slightly〔'slaɪtlɪ〕*adv.* 稍微；輕微地

　　　above〔ə'bʌv〕*prep.* 在⋯之上；高於⋯

　　　ability〔ə'bɪlətɪ〕*n.* 能力

TEST 100

【2015 高考北京卷】

TV Ears can help people with various degrees of hearing loss hear the television clearly. With TV Ears wireless technology, you set your own headset volume, while others hear the television at a volume level that's comfortable for them. You can even listen through the headset only and put the TV on mute if the situation calls for a quiet environment.

1. TV Ears helps you _____.

　　A. listen to TV without disturbing others.

　　B. change TV channels without difficulty.

TEST 100 詳解

【2015 高考北京卷】

TV Ears can help people *with various degrees of hearing loss* hear the television *clearly*. *With TV Ears wireless technology*, you set your own headset volume, **while** others hear the television *at a volume level **that**'s comfortable for them*. You can *even* listen *through the headset only* **and** put the TV *on mute* **if** *the situation calls for a quiet environment*.

電視耳可以幫助聽力喪失程度不同的人，清楚地聽到電視的聲音。利用電視耳的無線科技，你設定你自己的耳機音量，而其他人則用以他們自己感到舒適的音量聽電視。如果情況需要安靜的環境的話，你甚至可以將電視調到靜音模式，只透過耳機聽。

* various (ˈvɛrɪəs) *adj.* 各種不同的
degree (dɪˈgri) *n.* 程度；等級
hearing (ˈhɪrɪŋ) *n.* 聽力
loss (lɔs) *n.* 喪失；損害
clearly (ˈklɪrlɪ) *adv.* 清楚地；清晰地
wireless (ˈwaɪrlɪs) *adj.* 無線的
technology (tɛkˈnɑlədʒɪ) *n.* 科技
set (sɛt) *v.* 設定　　headset (ˈhɛdˌsɛt) *n.* 耳機

volume〔'vɑljəm〕*n.* 音量

level〔'lɛvl̩〕*n.* 程度；高度

comfortable〔'kʌmfətəbl̩〕*adj.* 舒服的；舒適的

through〔θru〕*prep.* 通過；透過

mute〔mjut〕*adj.* 無言的；沈默的；靜音的

situation〔ˌsɪtʃʊ'eʃən〕*n.* 狀態

call for 需要；要求　　quiet〔'kwaɪət〕*adj.* 安靜的

environment〔ɪn'vaɪrənmənt〕*n.* 環境

1. (**A**) TV Ears helps you _____.

　　 電視耳幫助你 _____。

　　 (A) listen to TV without disturbing others

　　　　 聽電視而不會打擾到其他人

　　 (B) change TV channels without difficulty

　　　　 毫無困難地變換電視頻道

　　 * disturb〔dɪ'stɝb〕*v.* 打擾

　　　 change〔tʃendʒ〕*v.* 改變；變換

　　　 channel〔'tʃænl̩〕*n.* 頻道

　　　 without difficulty 毫無困難地；輕鬆地

高三同學要如何準備「升大學考試」

　　考前該如何準備「學測」呢？「劉毅英文」的同學很簡單，只要熟讀每次的模考試題就行了。每一份試題都在7000字範圍內，就不必再背7000字了，從後面往前複習，越後面越重要，一定要把最後10份試題唸得滾瓜爛熟。根據以往的經驗，詞彙題絕對不會超出7000字範圍。每年題型變化不大，只要針對下面幾個大題準備即可。

準備「詞彙題」最佳資料：

背了再背，背到滾瓜爛熟，讓背單字變成樂趣。

考前不斷地做模擬試題就對了！

　　你做的題目愈多，分數就愈高。不要忘記，每次參加模考前，都要背單字、背自己所喜歡的作文。考壞不難過，勇往直前，必可得高分！

練習「模擬試題」，可參考「學習出版公司」最新出版的「7000字學測試題詳解」。我們試題的特色是：
①以「高中常用7000字」為範圍。②經過外籍專家多次校對，不會學錯。③每份試題都有詳細解答，對錯答案均有明確交待。

「克漏字」如何答題

　　第二大題綜合測驗（即「克漏字」），不是考句意，就是考簡單的文法。當四個選項都不相同時，就是考句意，就沒有文法的問題；當四個選項單字相同、字群排列不同時，就是考文法，此時就要注意到文法的分析，大多是考連接詞、分詞構句、時態等。「克漏字」是考生最弱的一環，你難，別人也難，只要考前利用這種答題技巧，勤加練習，就容易勝過別人。

準備「綜合測驗」（克漏字），可參考「學習出版公司」最新出版的「7000字克漏字詳解」。

本書特色：
1. 取材自大規模考試，英雄所見略同。
2. 不超出7000字範圍，不會做白工。
3. 每個句子都有文法分析。一目了然。
4. 對錯答案都有明確交待，列出生字，不用查字典。
5. 經過「劉毅英文」同學實際考過，效果極佳。

「文意選填」答題技巧

　　在做「文意選填」的時候，一定要冷靜。你要記住，一個空格一個答案，如果你不知道該選哪個才好，不妨先把詞性正確的選項挑出來，如介詞後面一定是名詞，選項裡面只有兩個名詞，再用刪去法，把不可能的選項刪掉。也要特別注意時間的掌控，已經用過的選項就劃掉，以免重複考慮，浪費時間。

準備「文意選填」，可參考「學習出版公司」最新出版的「7000字文意選填詳解」。

特色與「7000字克漏字詳解」相同，不超出7000字的範圍，有詳細解答。

「閱讀測驗」的答題祕訣

① 尋找關鍵字——整篇文章中，最重要就是第一句和最後一句，第一句稱為主題句，最後一句稱為結尾句。每段的第一句和最後一句，第二重要，是該段落的主題句和結尾句。從「主題句」和「結尾句」中，找出相同的關鍵字，就是文章的重點。因為美國人從小被訓練，寫作文要注重主題句，他們給學生一個題目後，要求主題句和結尾句都必須有關鍵字。

② 先看題目、劃線、找出答案、標題號——考試的時候，先把閱讀測驗題目瀏覽一遍，在文章中掃瞄和題幹中相同的關鍵字，把和題目相關的句子，用線畫起來，便可一目了然。通常一句話只會考一題，你畫了線以後，再標上題號，接下來，你找其他題目的答案，就會更快了。

③ 碰到難的單字不要害怕，往往在文章的其他地方，會出現同義字，因為寫文章的人不喜歡重覆，所以才會有難的單字。

④ 如果閱測內容已經知道，像時事等，你就可以直接做答了。

準備「閱讀測驗」，可參考「學習出版公司」最新出版的「7000字閱讀測驗詳解」，本書不超出7000字範圍，每個句子都有文法分析，對錯答案都有明確交待，單字註明級數，不需要再查字典。

「中翻英」如何準備

可參考劉毅老師的「英文翻譯句型講座實況DVD」，以及「文法句型180」和「翻譯句型800」。考前不停地練習中翻英，翻完之後，要給外籍老師改。翻譯題做得越多，越熟練。

「英文作文」怎樣寫才能得高分？

① 字體要寫整齊，最好是印刷體，工工整整，不要塗改。

② 文章不可離題，尤其是每段的第一句和最後一句，最好要有題目所說的關鍵字。

③ 不要全部用簡單句，句子最好要有各種變化，單句、複句、合句、形容詞片語、分詞構句等，混合使用。

④ 不要忘記多使用轉承語，像 *at present*（現在），*generally speaking*（一般說來），*in other words*（換句話說），*in particular*（特別地），*all in all*（總而言之）等。

⑤ 拿到考題，最好先寫作文，很多同學考試時，作文來不及寫，吃虧很大。但是，如果看到作文題目不會寫，就先寫測驗題，這個時候，可將題目中作文可使用的單字、成語圈起來，寫作文時就有東西寫了。但千萬記住，絕對不可以抄考卷中的句子，一旦被發現，就會以零分計算。

⑥ 試卷有規定標題，就要寫標題。記住，每段一開始，要內縮5或7個字母。

⑦ 可多引用諺語或名言，並注意標點符號的使用。文章中有各種標點符號，會使文章變得更美。

⑧ 整體的美觀也很重要，段落的最後一行字數不能太少，也不能太多。段落的字數要平均分配，不能第一段只有一、兩句，第二段一大堆。第一段可以比第二段少一點。

準備「英文作文」，可參考「學習出版公司」出版的：

☆ ☆ ☆ 全國最完整的文法書 ☆ ☆ ☆
文法寶典全集

劉 毅 編著 / 售價990元

　　這是一本想學好英文的人必備的工具書，作者積多年豐富的教學經驗，針對大家所不了解和最容易犯錯的地方，編寫成一本完整的文法書。

　　本書編排方式與眾不同，**第一篇就給讀者整體的概念**，再詳述文法中的細節部分，內容十分完整。文法說明以圖表為中心，一目了然，並且**務求深入淺出**。無論您在考試中或其他書中所遇到的任何不了解的問題，或是**您感到最煩惱的文法問題，查閱「文法寶典全集」均可迎刃而解。**

　　哪些副詞可修飾名詞或代名詞？(P.228)；什麼是介副詞？(P.543)；**哪些名詞可以當副詞用？**(P.100)；倒裝句(P.629)、省略句(P.644)等特殊構句，為什麼倒裝？為什麼省略？原來的句子是什麼樣子？在「文法寶典全集」裏都有詳盡的說明。

　　可見如果學文法不求徹底了解，反而成為學習英文的絆腳石，只要讀完本書，您必定信心十足，大幅提高對英文的興趣與實力。

極簡高中閱讀測驗
Make Reading Tests Easy

售價：280 元

主　　　編 / 劉　毅
發　行　所 / 學習出版有限公司　　　☎ (02) 2704-5525
郵 撥 帳 號 / 05127272 學習出版社帳戶
登　記　證 / 局版台業 *2179* 號
印　刷　所 / 文聯彩色印刷有限公司
台 北 門 市 / 台北市許昌街 17 號 6F　　☎ (02) 2331-4060
台灣總經銷 / 紅螞蟻圖書有限公司　　　☎ (02) 2795-3656
本公司網址 / www.learnbook.com.tw
電 子 郵 件 / learnbook@learnbook.com.tw

2020 年 10 月 1 日初版

4713269383932